DADDY
COME HOME

DADDY, COME HOME

THE TRUE STORY OF JOHN LENNON AND HIS FATHER

Pauline Lennon

A division of HarperCollins *Publishers*

AN ANGUS & ROBERTSON BOOK

Angus & Robertson (UK)
16 Golden Square, London, W1R 4BN
United Kingdom
Collins/Angus & Robertson Publishers Australia
A division of HarperCollins Publishers
(Australia) Pty Limited
Unit 4, Eden Park, 31 Waterloo Road,
North Ryde, NSW 2113, Australia
William Collins Publishers Ltd
31 View Road, Glenfield, Auckland 10,
New Zealand

First published in the United Kingdom
by Angus & Robertson (UK) in 1990
First published in Australia by
Collins/Angus & Robertson Australia in 1991

Text copyright © Pauline Lennon 1990

Typeset in Great Britain by The Wordshop
Rossendale, Lancs

Printed in Finland

British Library Cataloguing in Publication Data
Lennon, Pauline
    Daddy, come home: the true story of John Lennon
    and his father.
    1. Pop music. Lennon, John 1940–1980
    784.50092

ISBN 0 207 16996 9

FOREWORD

On the Primal Scream album (John Lennon/
Plastic Ono Band), which he recorded in 1970 on
completion of intensive psychotherapy, John
Lennon relives the emotional anguish of his early
separation from his parents and beseeches his
Daddy to come home.

This book explores the background to John's
traumatic childhood experiences and his
attempts to resolve his painful relationship with
his father.

Daddy Come Home is largely based on the text of Freddie Lennon's unpublished autobiography, without which this story could not have been told.

CONTENTS

	Prologue	9
1	Just Good Mates	11
2	Married to the Sea	33
3	Little Pal	55
4	Daddy, Come Home	76
5	The Prodigal Father	101
6	An Extraordinary Romance	124
7	There's Hope for Us Yet Dad	147
8	So Much Anger, So Much Pain	169
9	Like Father, Like Son	192
	Select Bibliography	209

PROLOGUE

As Freddie Lennon lay dying in a bleak public ward in Brighton General Hospital, a dismal building which has changed little in appearance since it was the district workhouse, he was astounded when the duty sister informed him that there was a long-distance telephone call for him from New York. Too weak to leave his hospital bed, he was even more astonished when the nurse wheeled the mobile telephone to his bedside and announced that the caller was the world-famous John Lennon – the son to whom he had not spoken for five years and with whom he had experienced so much conflict, misunderstanding and sorrow.

The ward was not so much for terminal care as for general surgical cases, so a number of the patients were sufficiently awake and alert to take a fascinated interest in the dramatic conversation which ensued between John and his father. Indeed many of them must have felt moved as they watched the expression of joy which lit up Freddie's thin face and the tears of happiness which rolled down his sunken cheeks as once again – and, he sensed, for the final time – he heard his son's voice.

'How you doing, whacker?' was John's cheery greeting in the Scouse style. 'I've been very worried about you.'

'Fifteen two,' responded Freddie with his favourite catchphrase, immediately ready to let bygones be bygones. 'It's great to hear from you, John.'

His son's message was one of reconciliation, a message which caused Freddie to choke back the sobs as he struggled to conceal his emotions from the curious eyes of the onlookers.

'I'm sorry I treated you the way I did, Dad,' were John's words. 'I should never have gone to the head shrink. It was a big mistake.'

'Forget it John, it's just bloody marvellous to talk to you again.'

Suddenly the nightmare of the past five years was over for Freddie, a nightmare which had begun on a wet October day when John, having recently undergone Janov regression therapy, had confronted his father with the anger he felt towards him. The months and months of indescribable heartache, born of the dreadful realization that his child hated him sufficiently to wish him dead, were now forgotten in the knowledge that John no longer bore him malice. He could die in peace.

1
JUST GOOD MATES

The reasons for John Lennon's lifelong bitterness towards his father were many and complex. But perhaps his greatest source of frustration was his total lack of knowledge of his paternal background, apparently denied him by his guardian, Aunt Mimi, and the seeming mystery surrounding the relationship between his father and his mother, Julia.

However, a few days after his father's death, John was to receive a typed copy of Freddie's autobiography, a revealing document which threw fascinating light on the enigma of his roots. Now for the first time he came to understand the magnetic and passionate attraction which formed the basis of his parents' unconventional, seventeen-year partnership. Now too he learned of the rich heritage of music and humour he had acquired from his Irish forebears. Now at long last he felt a true sense of belonging.

John's grandfather, John Lennon Senior, after whom the Beatle was named, was a happy-go-lucky, musically gifted Dubliner generally known as Jack, who sailed to New York as a member of a troupe of Kentucky Minstrels and toured the United States in the last half of the nineteenth century. Jack was a lad of tremendous spirit and enterprise, qualities undoubtedly passed on to his grandson, which enabled him to rise from humble beginnings to fulfil his ambition to become a travelling showman.

The Lennons of Dublin were Roman Catholics, and Jack's brother, having been ordained as a priest, had a

11

ministry in Wallasey, Cheshire. He eventually left the
Church for reasons which were never made public, although
rumour had it that his relationship with his housekeeper
may have been behind his dismissal.

While living in the USA Jack married and had a family,
but when his wife died he returned to Liverpool with his
youngest daughter, Mary. By now well into middle age, he
advertised for a housekeeper to care for himself and his
child.

The successful applicant was a certain Mary Maguire,
known to those who loved her as Polly. She was a handsome
young woman of quick wits, despite the fact that she had
never learned to read and write. Love soon blossomed, and
at an age when most men are expecting to become
grandfathers Jack married again and sired a further eight
children, all boys except for one daughter. The fourth boy
was the image of his father and was christened Alfred, later
to be known as Freddie.

As Jack believed in enjoying life he had few savings on his
return to Liverpool, which made it necessary for him to take
a job as a shipping clerk in order to support his new family.
He and Polly set up home in a tiny terraced house, two up,
two down, just off the main docks road in Toxteth, a
working-class area of Liverpool. Their new address was 27
Copperfield Street in the heart of 'Dickens Land', a group of
streets named after characters in Charles Dickens's novels.

Despite his straitened circumstances, Jack's spirits were
never down and whenever the chance arose for a spot of fun
he could always be relied upon to be the life and soul of the
party. He was a highly respected entertainer in the
Liverpool pubs, which provided him with an ideal platform
for his talents. His professional performances delighted the
regulars but did not always meet with his wife's approval –
such as the Christmas Eve when Jack hadn't turned up with
his wages and Polly was becoming anxious about her
Christmas shopping. She was quite sure where she could

find him, so throwing her shawl about her she made for the dockers' local, the Flat Iron. By that time the place was in full swing and Jack was doing one of his dramatic pieces. As Polly entered through the swing doors she found him standing on a table surrounded by the merry throng, finger pointing flamboyantly at the door as he shouted: 'Here entereth the woman now!' – to which she replied: 'Get home with your bloody wages.' The whole crowd fell off their stools with laughter, but all was well. He'd already been to the market and purchased the Christmas goose.

Jack was ever hopeful of winning a fortune and was constantly assuring his wife that before long he would have her 'farting against silk'. But his gregarious personality and generosity were such that he could never keep money in his pocket for long.

A favourite story in the family was that of the day Jack set out to place a ten-shilling bet on the first three horses in the Grand National. On the way out he met an old friend, down on his luck, and coughing painfully with a bad attack of bronchitis.

'Take this ten shillings,' was Jack's immediate response. 'Use it to fill up your larder and get yourself a good hot toddy.'

Everyone in the neighbourhood was overjoyed for Jack when his three horses came in, not realizing that the bet had never been placed, and naturally expected him to stand them a drink. Jack's unwillingness to disappoint them cost him a further ten shillings at the pub and a stern ticking off from his wife for acting so foolishly.

Freddie's mother Polly, although of Irish descent, was a Liverpudlian by birth and was endowed with the earthy wit, common sense and courage characteristic of most Scousers. Short, but of a broad, solid build, she fortunately possessed the muscle power necessary to cook, wash and clean for her husband and six surviving children in harsh financial circumstances, without any of the mod cons we now take for granted. Her smiling face, with its handsome Irish features and black hair drawn back into a bun, was a source of cheer and inspiration to all her relatives and neighbours. But most of all she was remembered for her quiet dignity which allowed her to rise above the difficult domestic situation she endured in common with most other Liverpudlian women just after the turn of the century.

Having lost two babies at birth who had been baptised in her husband's Roman Catholic faith, Polly was insistent that all her other children should be christened as Protestants. They duly were, although none of the family attended church and her true religion was that of fatalism – she staunchly accepted everything she was dealt in life without a trace of bitterness or self-pity. She was also quite free from jealousy of Jack's first wife, and insisted that a large portrait of the American beauty should take pride of place in the parlour.

Polly was gifted with what we would now term 'psychic ability'. She would sometimes have premonitions of events which would take place in the future and she also had the ability to see ghosts. No. 27 Copperfield Street was said to be haunted by a woman in white, reputedly responsible for doors suddenly shutting of their own accord. But Polly was the only member of the family ever to see the apparition.

Like most of their neighbours in the friendly docks community, the Lennons made the best of hard times and, in spite of her tough physical work, hand washing in the big dolly, manipulating the heavy mangle, or stretching a handful of food to feed eight hungry mouths, Polly made a comfortable little home for her family. There was always a brew of good strong tea available from the huge brown earthenware teapot kept by the hearth in the back kitchen, and most evenings the whole family would gather around the big wooden table to enjoy a traditional stew made from whatever scraps Polly could lay her hands on. By creating infinite variations of this 'Scouse', as the stew was known,

Liverpudlian women became adept at making a little go a very long way. But despite Polly's efforts to keep her children's bellies full, the food was not of the highest nutritional quality and, as for many families at that time, rickets was a problem amongst the children.

Freddie, the fourth surviving son born to Jack and Polly in 1912, was badly affected by rickets and his legs were so weak that the doctor ordered him to wear 'irons' to give them some support. The growth lost was nevertheless considerable; his legs were some four inches shorter than they should have been, and he never grew taller than five feet four inches.

There may not have been much money in the family, but of fun, laughter and music there was plenty, and Freddie's early years were spent learning the songs and impersonations which had formed part of his father's repertoire in the United States and which Jack was constantly performing. One of his earliest memories was that of sitting on his father's knee accompanying him in singing 'Ave Maria', tears rolling down both their faces.

The good times came to an end for Freddie at the age of seven, when Jack died leaving a widow and six children. Freddie's last memory of his father was of being led upstairs to bid him goodbye and of seeing him laid out on the bed with two pennies on his eyes. For Freddie, his father's death meant the final end of any real family life. In dire financial straits, Polly considered it prudent to accept the offer of places for two of her children at the Bluecoat Orphanage. And it was here that Freddie was duly despatched as a boarder, together with his sister Edith.

The Liverpool Bluecoat School, founded in 1714, was well known throughout the north of England and children able to obtain places there were considered extremely fortunate to gain such a good start in life. To Freddie, however, the parting from his mother whom he idolized,

15

and the sudden ejection into the big bad world, seemed nothing less than the greatest misfortune possible.

The school derived its name from the uniform which all the boys had been required to wear since the school's foundation, and which comprised a close-fitting blue jacket with silver buttons and tails, worn over blue trousers and a silver waistcoat. The outfit was completed by a tippet worn at the neck, reminiscent of the legal profession.

The homesick young Freddie did obtain some solace, however, through the friendship of Jackie Bond, an older boy who was the captain of the school football team and who took the youngster under his wing and appointed him team mascot on account of his unusually small size. Jackie Bond was eventually to become a schoolmaster at Quarry Bank High School, where his patience was to be sorely tried by the school's most non-conformist pupil, Freddie's son John Lennon.

The rules and regulations of the orphanage were a far cry from the high-spirited, devil-may-care atmosphere that Freddie's father had created at home. Although music was taught at the school, the curriculum was classical and conservative and the extrovert street music with which Freddie had been brought up was frowned upon as not respectable.

Although there was little opportunity to indulge his love of entertaining under the auspices of the Bluecoat School, the holidays allowed Freddie a little more scope. He found he could soon summon an audience from his young friends in Copperfield Street, who would willingly pay their Saturday pennies to hear Freddie's repertoire of songs, Charlie Chaplin impersonations and the latest hits played on the harmonica.

Brass bands represented another form of street music in the North of England at that time and held a special fascination for young Freddie. Many was the occasion when he would follow the band right to the outskirts of the city, totally absorbed in the music and drama of the procession, to find himself utterly lost. Many was the spanking he received from Polly following his return home courtesy of a helpful 'bobby'.

One particular summer holiday an important opportunity arose for Freddie. As a special treat he was taken by his elder brother, Sydney, to a show at the Empire Theatre in Liverpool entitled *Will Murray's Gang*, which was a well-known children's spectacular of that time. Freddie was fascinated by the music, the lights and the costumes, and most of all by the leading boy, resplendent in top hat and tails, and by the time the show was over he was well and truly stage-struck. So when, at the final curtain, Will Murray himself appeared and invited parents whose children had any talent to visit him backstage, Freddie, with his natural self-confidence, urged Sydney to introduce him.

When Will Murray enquired of young Freddie what he could do, he boldly claimed, 'I'm better than your leading boy.'

Scrutinizing his Bluecoat uniform, Murray replied, 'You're an orphan boy, aren't you?'

'Yes, sir,' said Freddie, adding quickly, 'I'm nearly fourteen.'

'Well, let's see what you can do,' urged the producer. Sitting down at the piano he began to play 'We All Like to be Beside the Seaside', whereupon Freddie entered into the number with gusto, arms and legs accompanying him. Murray was impressed, and when Sydney had explained that their mother could neither read nor write he allowed Sydney himself to fill in a temporary form engaging Freddie, for what the rest of the family imagined would be instant stardom.

As the Bluecoat School shared custody of the child, permission was required from the orphanage before Freddie could be released from his schooling to join the troupe. This they refused to give, viewing the whole episode with some contempt. Sick with disappointment, young Freddie found the lure of the bright lights too much for his rebellious spirit. So, bidding his mother goodbye in a farewell letter, he packed his bag and joined the Murray Gang on the road for their next venue, in Glasgow.

All did not end well, however, and Freddie paid a high price for his adventure. A few days later he was accompanied back to Liverpool by a stern-faced Bluecoat master and subjected to public humiliation before the whole of the assembled orphanage.

'So you thought you were going to be a star?' taunted the scornful master. 'And which part were they going to give you, Tom Thumb or perhaps one of the Seven Dwarfs?' he continued, scathingly drawing attention to Freddie's short-ness of stature.

His sense of self-worth annihilated, Freddie dropped the idea of a career in showbusiness, although he continued to sing for fun and to entertain his friends and family. It was also the first time his short height had been drawn attention to in a derogatory way, and the blow to his confidence gave him a complex about his size which he never really conquered.

His dreams of stardom shattered, when the time came for Freddie to leave the Bluecoat School his thoughts turned next to the possibility of going to sea. He loved nothing better than to stand on the Pier Head watching the big cruisers sail into the busy passenger port of Liverpool, imagining the exotic locations from which they hailed, and if a career on the stage was impossible, then a life at sea seemed the next best option.

Around this time, shortly before sailing on his first ship as a bell boy, Freddie was to meet his first girlfriend, Julia Stanley, future mother of John, and the only woman he was to love for the next four decades. Freddie was just sixteen and five foot nothing, but his Irish good looks, jet-black hair

18

and not least his Celtic eloquence gave him a better than average chance with the female sex.

Julia was one year younger, a gloriously pretty girl with long red hair and a face and figure which resembled Ginger Rogers. Like the film star, she too loved to dance and spent most of her spare time practising new steps at the local dance hall or watching musicals at the movies. Her only flaw was severe short sight, later passed on to John. But as she discarded her glasses as soon as she left school, no one was ever aware of her poor eye-sight, including Freddie.

Her first job on leaving school was in a firm of printers and stationers in Paradise Street, although after about a year she was sacked as a result of her over-active sense of humour and indulgence in pranks. But the cloud was not without its silver lining, as some months later she was successful in obtaining work as a cinema usherette. She started at the Trocadero, where she was able to watch her favourite film stars to her heart's content and lose herself in the fantasy world of the big screen.

Julia's good looks and high spirits attracted many admirers, not least the manager of the Trocadero who was forever attempting to woo her by leaving in her locker presents of nylons, which were difficult to obtain at that time. Others were prepared to go to quite extraordinary lengths to win her affection. One of them, the son of a wealthy confectioner of some esteem in Liverpool, was known locally as Francis the Umbrella Man due to the fact that he was never seen without his large black umbrella. Eventually driven to distraction by his passion, he felt moved to kneel down in the middle of the London Road, a busy Liverpool thoroughfare, where he vowed his undying love for Julia while police attempted to drag him to safety.

Whereas the Lennon family was male-dominated, the Stanley family consisted almost entirely of females. There were five children, all girls, christened Julia, Ann, Harriet, Betty and Mary.

At first sight their parents seemed extraordinarily ill matched. Anne Stanley (née Millward) was a graceful woman, kind and patient, from a respectable and refined family background. In contrast George Stanley, known to one and all as 'Pop', was a much more rough and ready character who had spent most of his life in the navy and whose language, when he was inebriated, was highly colourful regardless of the company.

But Anne and George Stanley shared a status-conscious outlook on life and lofty ambitions for their five daughters. Betty was the first to fulfil their high hopes, having married 'well' to a Captain Charles Parkes with whom she had settled into a luxurious home. The Stanleys themselves lived in a flat in Berkeley Street in a more upmarket area of Liverpool than the Lennons' humble terraced house in Copperfield Street. But the two families differed not so much in terms of class as in terms of aspiration.

Of the five girls, all strikingly pretty, Harriet, Ann and Betty took after their mother with their gentleness and placidity, whilst Mary and Julia inherited the toughness and assertiveness of their father. Mary, first nicknamed Mimi by Betty's little boy Stanley Parkes, was the most ambitious and strong-willed of the daughters, whereas Julia was perhaps the zaniest and the most frivolous; Mimi had a burning desire to get on in life whilst Julia, totally lacking in ambition, found an outlet for her energy by having a good time. Nevertheless it was Julia who was the closest to her father and he to her, and it seemed that she was his obvious favourite. While Mimi often appeared to disapprove of Pop, Julia was always ready to defend him most loyally against one and all, including her mother.

The first meeting between Freddie and Julia took place while they were still youngsters, in Sefton Park, where all the boys and girls in the neighbourhood went for their Sunday outing. It was the custom for the sexes to divide into two groups and to stroll past one another, eyeing each other up for a prospective date – a ritual which became known as 'the monkey rack'.

One Sunday, having donned his best suit and bowler hat, Freddie made his usual way to Sefton Park. It wasn't a particularly nice day, sunless and drizzling slightly, and the 'rack' was virtually deserted. Optimistically he sauntered down to the lakeside where, to his surprise, sitting on a park bench was a girl, all alone and looking as cheerless as the weather. He paused to put a cigarette in his holder – by permission of his brother Sydney he was now smoking Woodbines, a habit which was to persist until the end of his life.

He was initially puzzled when the girl burst out laughing when he politely enquired, 'Do you mind if I sit down?' but in retrospect it seemed obvious that the sight of a tiny young lad with a bowler perched on his ears, elaborately waving a cigarette holder, must have been a fairly hilarious sight. Undaunted, he sat down beside her, offering her a cigarette – which she refused – and enquired as to the cause of her merriment.

'Your hat,' she replied between bursts of high-pitched laughter. 'It looks ridiculous!'

'OK,' he remarked indignantly and, snatching the offending item from his head, threw it far across the lake. This action only roused Julia to more vigorous peals of laughter in which Freddie soon joined, whereupon they promptly became friends, exchanging names and promising to meet the next evening for a visit to the cinema.

It soon became obvious that they were two of a kind, sharing an irrepressible and slightly crazy sense of humour and a total lack of respect for convention. And perhaps it was their tendency to blow raspberries at establishment values which drew them closest together.

The friendship was nurtured during the months that followed by long walks in the parks. They passed the time by wheeling Betty's baby, Stanley, whiling away the hours chattering and joking, usually at the expense of others, and generally playing the fool. The butt of their humour tended to be Julia's sister Mimi or Freddie's elder brother Sydney, who each aspired towards the sort of bourgeois respectability which they held in such disdain.

However, the month of March saw the first of many partings, when Freddie was lucky enough to fulfil his ambition of obtaining a position as a bell boy and gained a job on the Cunard passenger liner the SS *Montrose*. Unemployment was rife in Liverpool in 1930 and there were invariably several hundred applicants for every vacancy. Given the hordes of men and boys who besieged the ship company offices whenever recruits were needed, either luck or influence was required to stand any chance of being selected. In Freddie's case it was his Bluecoat education which earned him the post.

At about that time the shipping companies were beginning to develop the idea of short Mediterranean cruises to suit the pocket of the thousands of available customers who had neither the time nor the money for longer cruises to the Bahamas or around the world. So Freddie's first trip to sea was in the nature of a trial cruise, listed in fact as a scholars' cruise – nine days of sunshine and lessons for a pound a day.

As it turned out, the scholars all proved to be screaming, yelling girls, average age sixteen, determined to enjoy themselves in every sense of the word in the Mediterranean sun. Indeed it was the firm opinion of the whole crew that at least 50 per cent of the young ladies would have cause for concern, as well as happy memories, as a result of their 'scholars' cruise. And Freddie himself came very close to losing his virginity when a gaggle of giggling girl pupils leaped upon him, dragged him into the cabin facing the chief steward's office, and stripped him stark naked! The timely entrance of the chief steward denied him the chance of discovering what came next.

It was on this first trip that he made the acquaintance of a lad by the name of Jacko, a curly-haired replica of himself with the same mischievous glint in his eye. Jacko and Lennie, as Freddie was called at sea, soon became the best of mates and throughout their career were known as 'the terrible twins' on account of their identical delight in outrageous pranks.

But despite the fun the days were long, and the boys found they were expected to work through from six until three without a break. A siesta followed, in preparation for the evening session which began at five and often continued until late. However, despite the hard work and long hours young Freddie was overwhelmed by the excitement and glamour of life on the cruisers. And naturally, on disembarkation at Liverpool, his first thought was to renew his friendship with Julia and recount all the humorous stories he had to tell about the voyage.

Having presented himself at her door in full regalia in expectation of a salutatory 'How nice you look', Freddie's pride was somewhat wounded when he was met with peals of Julia's characteristic delirious laughter. Slinking home to change, he decided not to see her again, but the magnetic attraction which had sprung up between them soon reunited the young friends and before long they were laughing and joking together once more.

Nevertheless the sea proved to be an even greater attraction for Freddie, and after six weeks' shore leave he packed his bag, bid Julia farewell and headed once again for the docks. Freddie found it hard to understand Julia's attitude to his career at sea. It was true that she was always pleased to see him whenever he returned to Liverpool, and despite her good looks and popularity she never entertained any other serious boyfriends. But on the other hand she never showed any sign of being upset when he went back to sea. Unlike most of the other stewards' girlfriends she would never go to the docks to see him off on a voyage, and she would usually restrict her farewells to a sulky 'See you then' and maybe a peck on the cheek.

Neither did she reply to any of Freddie's letters, despite the fact that he wrote regularly to her, initially every day, but always from each port of call. Like John after her, Julia disliked letter-writing, giving the excuse that she 'couldn't be bothered', although she enjoyed receiving letters and reading them.

In reality she had fallen head over heels in love with the young sailor and was deeply unhappy about the inevitable partings. But her rebellious spirit did not allow her to show her feelings and she simply pretended that she didn't care.

For his part, Freddie was totally devoted to Julia from the moment of their first meeting, although there can be no doubt that many opportunities for affairs with the passengers existed for stewards. The cruise liners were particularly popular with single women of all ages eager for the no-strings-attached thrill of a shipboard romance, and many of them succumbed to the virile charms of the muscular and bronzed young stewards. Indeed, with a passenger list of anything from one thousand to fifteen hundred, the crew, especially the waiters, were never in doubt that another heart-rending romance under the starry sky would lighten the burden of their sixteen hours' toil. So sure were they of a conquest that the bolder boys would even pick out their prospective partners for the voyage from the passenger list before the 'bloods' (ship's jargon for passengers) had even joined the ship.

Inevitably Freddie himself was repeatedly propositioned although he usually managed to withdraw unscathed from the fray, leaving the action to his mate Jacko, and remarkably he remained faithful to Julia from the beginning to the end of their relationship. The most persistent of his admirers was a plump American widow of middling years who became so besotted with the cute young Scouser that she actually asked him to marry her, promising all kinds of luxuries and monetary inducements if he would only return with her to the States. His response to the wealthy matron was the one he usually gave to extract himself from such situations. 'I'm sorry but I've got a girlfriend at home in Liverpool – and I love her.' And he meant it.

The friendship between Freddie and Julia continued in a spasmodic pattern for the next four or five years under the critical watch of Pop Stanley. Julia was the apple of her father's eye, and he had high hopes of her marrying 'well' like her sister Betty.

For this reason her relationship with young Alfred Lennon had sadly disappointed him. In his eyes the happy-go-lucky, penniless young sailor was entirely the wrong company for Julia. Not only was he lacking in prospects but he was also lacking in any desire to 'get on' in life and seemed to spend most of his free time frittering away his earnings and generally acting the fool. What was more, he came from the 'wrong' side of town and he had even heard it rumoured that his mother was unable to read and write.

Despite her affection for her father, it was precisely his opposition to Freddie which made the relationship so attractive to Julia. Totally disdainful of convention, she had no intention of marrying simply for status, and her friendship with Freddie had initially represented a gesture of contempt for the trappings of respectability. But she was not entirely successful in breaking through the class barrier and showed no interest in making the acquaintance of the rest of the Lennon family. In fact only once did she meet Freddie's mother – and that was not until after John was born.

In terms of wilfulness Julia and her father were of the same mould, and the more headstrong she became about continuing to see the young sailor the more Pop Stanley determined to try to break up the affair. The worst of the showdowns occurred at a weekend party at Betty's home at

Rock Ferry, attended by the whole of the Stanley family apart from Mimi. The usual prelude to these Scouse parties was that the gentlemen would retire to the local pub and leave the ladies to become better acquainted for the night's revelries, which often continued until the early hours.

On this particular occasion, due to lack of funds, Freddie did not join the men in their exodus to the pub and stayed behind with the women, who were fixing a loudspeaker from the radiogram in the lounge to the drawing room. Upon the return of the jubilant men, because of his more or less sober state Freddie went to join the ladies in the drawing room. On his way he tripped across a length of unseen flex and brought the loudspeaker crashing down to the floor.

'You stupid little bugger!' bellowed out the thunderous voice of Pop Stanley, and his ocean-going obscenities rent the happy atmosphere to such an extent that Julia's mother Anne, cool as ever, was forced to close the lounge doors.

Freddie retreated to the kitchen, followed by Pop who slammed the door behind him and made to strike the youngster. 'I've damn well had enough of you!' he roared, but checked himself as he heard Julia's voice screaming, 'Don't hit him, father, please.'

Captain Parkes, Betty's husband, appeared, and in his efficient manner managed to calm everyone down. 'Listen, Freddie, the best thing you can do is to find yourself a cargo ship and lie low for a while until Pop has cooled down.'

Meanwhile a taxi had been summoned to take Freddie back home, but in spite of her father's protests Julia insisted on leaving at the same time. It was about one o'clock on the Sunday morning when they arrived at Julia's home in Berkeley Street, so after a cup of coffee and a smoke they lay down on the settee and instantly fell asleep.

They were aroused at about eight in the morning, not by church bells but by George Stanley, a little more sober but just as belligerent in mood. At the sight of the pair on the settee his temper exploded once again.

'You'll bloody well get out of my house!' he raved, 'I thought I told you to leave my daughter alone.'

'Your daughter's old enough to make up her own mind about her friends,' was Freddie's response, but he was cut short by the entrance of Captain Parkes who had followed in his car, sensing further trouble.

'Freddie, you'll be pleased to hear I've found you a job on a whaling ship which sails tonight for about two years,' he announced, news which was greeted with obvious delight by Pop Stanley, who immediately remarked that Julia would probably be married by the time Freddie returned.

Aware that a two-year trip on a whaler could set up a man financially for life, Freddie was strongly tempted to accept the offer, so he set off home to pack his bags and break the news to Polly. But when he met Julia later that afternoon, what she had to say caused him to change his plans.

'Mother told me that it was Pop who asked Captain Parkes to find you a long voyage,' she confided. 'You know Father wants to keep us apart, and this is his way of doing so.'

Adamant that he would not submit to this ploy, Freddie marched down to Berkeley Street and informed George Stanley what he could do with his offer.

'Right then, Lennon, never darken my doorstep again,' was the old man's response, and for some months afterwards the young lovers were obliged to meet in secret.

There is nothing like a spot of parental opposition to strengthen the bonds of a love affair, and the setback brought Julia and Freddie much closer together. The romance was also helped on its way by a prolonged spell of shore leave, as Freddie was unable to obtain a ship for some months.

Although they would often cuddle up in bed together, Freddie had great respect for his beautiful girlfriend and despite a good deal of petting they never actually made love.

27

Nevertheless the question of marriage had not yet arisen and both of them seemed satisfied with their relationship as it stood. More than anything else they were just good mates, and like all good mates they loved nothing better than to clown around together and have fun.

To Julia's parents, however, the question of marriage was an important one, and Pop Stanley in particular was anxious to see his highly eligible daughter happily settled. Freddie was the last person he would have wished for Julia, but she had proved that her heart was set on him and there was nothing more he could do to dissuade her without losing her affection. If Freddie refused to free her to find a new boyfriend, then it was about time he declared his intentions towards her.

Aware that pressure was building up, Freddie was hardly surprised when he was formally invited to tea by Mrs Anne Stanley one Saturday afternoon. Unlike Pop Stanley, his wife had a soft spot for Freddie and always referred to him as a 'little gentleman' despite her spouse's opinions. Her obvious embarrassment when he finally arrived for tea suggested to Freddie that she had something to say that he probably wouldn't like.

Following some uneasy small talk, Mrs Stanley eventually blurted out, 'Are you two ever going to get married?' whereupon Julia burst out laughing, much to her mother's disgust.

'Can't you ever be serious?' she chided. 'I want to know if you've thought about getting married and settling down.'

Freddie valiantly restrained himself from repeating Julia's mistake and feebly answered, 'We've never discussed it', sensing what her mother was leading up to.

'Well, Pop thinks that after ten years it's about time you gave it some serious thought.' And turning to address Freddie personally she went on to inform him, in her very gentle manner, that Pop was no longer against his marrying Julia but on the contrary was disturbed that he seemed to be

28

making no effort to do so.

'You see, Freddie, you're not only wasting her time but you're also preventing her from finding herself a husband.' This set Julia off again in hopeless spasms of mirth in which her mother was eventually forced to join, although she added gravely, 'You'd better make up your minds soon. Pop's going away for a month but wants a definite answer one way or the other when he returns – or else.'

The following day was a Sunday, which gave them plenty of time to discuss their plans. Freddie was still unemployed, neither of them had any savings, so there was no prospect of a home of their own, and the future didn't seem particularly bright. As usual, however, they just couldn't be serious, and it wasn't until they were about to say goodnight that they realized they still hadn't arrived at any decisions.

'I know what it is,' said Julia, flashing her eyes mischievously and tossing back her fiery locks. 'You're scared to put up the banns.'

'I bet you I'll do it tomorrow,' was Freddie's defiant reply. And to everyone's surprise he did just that.

During the following three weeks, as they awaited the day of the wedding, they hardly discussed their future at all, and when they did it was never responsibly. Neither had told their families of their intentions, hoping to surprise them with a *fait accompli*, and of course Julia had never met Freddie's mother or any other members of his family.

But on the Friday before the happy day, Freddie was obliged through lack of funds to inform Polly of his plans. Normally he handed over most of his dole money to help out with the housekeeping, but this week he needed some extra to pay the registrar for the licence. Certain that it was just one of his jokes, Polly simply didn't believe him; nor was she convinced the next morning when he arose bright and early to press his one and only suit and polish his shoes.

Julia had gone to work as usual, having arranged the

previous night to meet Freddie outside the Bolton Street register office behind the Adelphi Hotel, accompanied by one of her friends who worked at the same cinema.

Freddie left his perplexed mother at about ten o'clock and made his way to the Eagle in Paradise Street in the hope that he might find one of his mates there to stand as a witness. He waited until nearly twelve, but nobody he knew well enough turned up, so in desperation he phoned his brother Sydney at work and begged him to meet him within five minutes outside the Adelphi.

Sydney was an ambitious and hard-working individual, steadily forging his way to the top in the mens' outfitting business. He and Freddie were just about as unalike as they could be: whereas he made a point of actively courting status and respectability, these social distinctions were positive anathema to Freddie. Indeed, the two brothers' relationship was very similar to that between Julia and her elder sister Mimi, who also totally opposed one another in their attitude to convention and social standing. In Sydney's eyes Freddie was wasting the good start he had received at the Bluecoat School, and he would often chastise him for his devil-may-care attitude with the comment: 'If I'd had your education I wouldn't have thrown it away like you've done.'

Having awkwardly made his excuses to his superiors at the shop, Sydney was hardly in a mood to join in the fun when he was greeted by his anxious younger brother.

'You're in no position to be getting married – what the hell are you going to do? Where will you live?' was his curt greeting, to which Freddie calmly replied, 'We'll get by.'

It was twelve-thirty before Julia arrived, accompanied by her friend, but as the register office didn't close until one o'clock they were just in time for the ceremony. Sydney, by now striving valiantly to maintain a happy demeanour, came to the rescue by providing lunch and drinks at a nearby pub known as the 'Big House'.

The newly-weds spent their honeymoon in the Forum

Cinema, now renamed the Odeon. The film was *Dr Barnardo's Homes* starring the young Mickey Rooney, and Freddie spent most of the time telling Julia that it wasn't as good as the orphanage where he himself had been educated.

With no home of their own to return to, it was straight back to their parents' house that night. Before making his way to 'Coppie', as they nicknamed Copperfield Street, Freddie left Julia at the corner of Berkeley Street at her request in case Pop had arrived back home. She thought it better to be by herself when she told him of her marriage.

Polly Lennon was never surprised at Freddie's slightly crazy antics. He reminded her too much of the unpredictable Jack, and she would often fondly confide to him: 'Your father will never be dead for me while you're alive.' So when the proud young husband made his triumphant entrance she merely boxed his ears affectionately.

Julia had fewer problems than she had expected in breaking the news to her own parents. Although her mother commented, 'You'll have more dinner times than dinners', both she and George were at least relieved that the pair were finally hitched and that Julia had at last achieved what she seemed to want.

But in many ways things were really no different for the young lovers from the way they had been before the marriage. With nowhere private to call their own, they hadn't even had a chance to consummate the union before Freddie was summoned back to sea again by the Merchant Navy Pool. Surprisingly, however, Pop Stanley came to their rescue.

Disembarking at Liverpool Docks a few weeks later, Freddie was astonished at the sight of Julia, dressed in her usherette's uniform, who for the first and only time in her life had come to meet his ship. As soon as she caught sight of Freddie she burst into excited laughter and blurted out, 'We're going home.'

31

Freddie was highly perplexed, especially when they boarded a bus for the suburb of Woolton, but he was unable to prise any information from Julia except that they were 'going home'. As they alighted at Penny Lane she giggled, 'This is it', and taking Freddie by the hand began to lead him up Church Road. For a moment he thought he was returning to the Bluecoat School which was located close by, but Julia turned into Newcastle Road and, stopping at No. 9, inserted the key, opened the door and politely bade him enter.

Freddie's astonishment was entirely without bounds when he was greeted by a beaming Mr and Mrs Stanley, who came forward to welcome him to his new home. After a warm hug from Mrs Stanley, he nearly collapsed when his father-in-law approached him with outstretched hand and said, 'Glad to see you, son.'

Anxious to do his very best for his favourite daughter, and now that the other girls were married or had left home, it had been Pop Stanley's idea to move from the flat in Berkeley Street to a house big enough to accommodate himself, his wife, Julia and Freddie. It was a comfortable, well-furnished home and apart from the fact that they all ate together, the newlyweds had plenty of privacy and lots of time to themselves.

When Freddie returned to 'Coppie' the next day to break the news to his mother and to collect a few of his things, Polly's reaction was her usual laconic observation: 'Trust him to fall into it, he'll always get by.'

2
MARRIED TO THE SEA

John Lennon was conceived on a cold January afternoon in 1940 on the kitchen floor at 9 Newcastle Road, Liverpool. Having been away at sea over Christmas Freddie docked on 5 January, radiant with expectation at the prospect of seeing Julia again. Despite the undoubted excitement of life at sea, every time they were reunited he felt that same thrill he had experienced on their first meeting.

Although Julia and Freddie had already known each other for some twelve years, the glow of their passion for each other had not yet dimmed, and at that time the long periods of parting still made every homecoming seem like a honeymoon. Since Julia never came to the docks, their reunion would inevitably take place in the house, and such was the spontaneity of their feelings for each other that they would invariably make love there and then.

A trip aboard the *Empress of Canada* from 30 July to 1 November meant that Freddie was not home for John's birth, although one month's shore leave shortly afterwards enabled him to get to know his young son. The name John was chosen by Freddie after his own father, whom he had loved dearly but who had died when he was only seven. Julia's choice for his second name was Winston – inspired perhaps by patriotism or perhaps by her love of the ridiculous.

It was now wartime and much of Freddie's shore leave during the early months of John's life was spent fire-watching at the docks, or, when the bombing was at its height, in the air raid shelter with Julia, her parents and baby John. Freddie was delighted to find that George Stanley's bark was much worse than his bite and they actually managed to get on well together. In fact, Pop was absolutely over the moon when his favourite daughter Julia made him a granddad again. He saw very little of his other two grandchildren, Leila (Harriet's daughter) and Stanley (Betty's son), especially now that Betty lived 'over the water' – across the Mersey in Wallasey.

Shore leave was short and infrequent, however, and the increasing impact of the war meant that Freddie's trips at sea were becoming longer. In fact his log book bears witness that from 1 August 1940 until 13 January 1944 he spent only three months at home in Liverpool.

Now that John had arrived it soon became obvious that Julia was less tolerant of the long periods apart, and Freddie began to sense a change in her attitude towards him. The continual laughing and joking which had formed the basis of their relationship was starting to wear a bit thin, and for the first time Julia began to put pressure on Freddie to look for work ashore after the war.

'But you know I've no talent for anything else, pet,' would be his unvarying response. 'It's my whole life.'

'If you really loved me you'd put me first. You'd promise to pack in the sea after the war,' she would complain. 'The fact is, Freddie, that you're married to the sea and, sooner or later you're going to have to choose between us.'

For Freddie the dilemma was a difficult one. He loved Julia madly, as he had loved her from the first day he had set eyes on her, and it was tremendously gratifying to know that she missed him while he was away and wanted him with her always. But there was another side of him which was in desperate need of freedom, which needed to keep constantly on the move, and which caused him to feel immensely frustrated if he felt himself to be pinned down. As a typical Sagittarian, Freddie Lennon was a travelling man, like his father before him, and in order to settle down ashore it would have been necessary for him to sell his soul, something he was not prepared to do. From the early days spent watching the big liners at Liverpool's Pier Head, Freddie's dream had been to see the world and it was work on the cruisers, firstly on the Mediterranean circuit and later on the Atlantic run, which gave him the chance to do just that.

A life at sea had tremendous attractions for an adventurous young lad, not just in terms of sight-seeing but also by virtue of the scintillating social life it offered. The night life in the ports of call was a fascinating and compelling ritual for merchant sailors, and was undoubtedly one of the reasons why Freddie, like so many others, became addicted to the sea. There was something irresistible about the bright lights and the places of entertainment where the booze and the excitement flowed all night.

For Freddie, however, the main attraction of ship life lay in the scope it gave him to exploit his showbiz talents, and he soon gained a name for the outstanding entertainment he would set up during each trip in the crew's bar, known to passengers and sailors alike as the Pig and Whistle. In fact, such was the success and renown of these shows that on most ships the passengers would insist on being allowed to crowd in and share the fun.

The procedure was usually much the same. Every first night at sea a conference would be held to make arrangements for the entertainments, at which Freddie, assisted by his good mate Jacko, would normally be given the task of recruiting the talent. He was also responsible for compering the shows and for rendering the occasional 'hot number' or sometimes a tear-jerking classic.

The gays, who made up a fair proportion of the stewards, represented the backbone of the entertainment proceedings and gave Freddie plenty of material from which to devise the shows. For the gays themselves the concerts provided an excellent opportunity to don full drag without condemnation – homosexuality being much less acceptable to the public at that time than it is now. But there was little prejudice against the gays on the ships, where they were well accepted and in many cases well loved.

There was always one of the older gays who would acquire the name of 'Mother', and a ritual highlight of the entertainment during each trip was the staging of a wedding for 'Mother' with full regalia and wedding feast. Somehow or other the boys always managed to provide a banquet with food 'borrowed' from the passengers' supplies – turkey, sandwiches and hors d'oeuvres – which they were usually successful in snatching, often with the co-operation of the chief steward, such was the popularity of the event. The ship's baker would prepare a special wedding cake, the tiers of which were made from blocks of wood and the cutting of which by 'Mother' would nearly upset the lavish spread which adorned the tables.

Amongst the 'bloods' it was usually the men only who were allowed into the Pig and Whistle to witness the hilarity of the ceremony, on account of the outrageously camp backchat. On one occasion, however, the ladies threatened to storm the Pig if they weren't allowed in; naturally they laughed much louder at the blue jokes than did the men.

On the night of the wedding the Pig and Whistle would be packed to suffocating with passengers, firemen and sailors, all quite happy to rub shoulders with one another. 'Mother' and her two bridesmaids, dressed in full drag, would always look radiant, but had to compete for laughs with the bridegroom who appeared in top hat and tails without any trousers, and the vicar who wore only a pair of striped shorts and a dog collar.

It was shortly after Julia's ultimatum that Freddie met Major Eric Maschwitz of 'Balalaika' fame, who was one of the passengers on the *Moreton Bay*. Because of his vast knowledge of stage and screen productions, Freddie asked Maschwitz to organize the ship's concert party in his place.

Impressed by his talents, the Major gave Lennie the star part in the show and devised a special act for him, based on music and comedy. He incorporated Freddie's favourite Hitler caricature but improved on it with his professional touches, such as providing a platform with a glass of water upon it which of course ended up knocked over one of the stormtroopers whom he arranged to have standing on either side of him. And when Freddie arrived at his final violent outburst he insisted he should fall frothing at the mouth in a crumpled heap, to be carried out by his aides.

Naturally Freddie asked the maestro about his prospects of invading show business, but he was actually sorry he did, for Maschwitz killed what little hope he had left, although he did reinforce his confidence in his ability to entertain.

'You're pretty good, Lennie,' he informed Freddie. 'In fact, if I or anyone else in my position had discovered you about ten years ago, you would certainly have made the grade. But,' he added, shaking his head sadly, 'by the time this bloody war's finished it will be too late to start.' And that was the final confirmation for Freddie that a life in show business was apparently not for him.

Nevertheless Freddie was beginning to fulfil his ambitions for promotion, and in September 1942 he gained the plum job of saloon steward – ship's jargon for head waiter – on the *Moreton Bay*. Bubbling with excitement as he announced the news, he found it hard to understand Julia's apparent indifference.

'Aren't you pleased for me, pet?' he asked, lifting her from her feet and swinging her around the room.

'You know the way I feel,' was her quiet reply. 'I want you home, home with me and John.'

'But it's wartime, pet. I just couldn't be at home right now, however much I wanted to be.'

'And after the war?' she pressed him.

'We'll see, darling, we'll see.'

Mimi, on the other hand, was absolutely thrilled about

Freddie's new appointment, and riled Julia by constantly reminding her what a wonderful husband she had and how proud she should be of him. Whereas Julia was totally lacking in ambition on Freddie's behalf, Mimi looked forward to the day when her brother-in-law might become a chief steward and urged her sister to be grateful for the extra money that Freddie was now able to give her.

The next trip was to be a long one, however, so Mimi attempted to cheer up her sister by suggesting that she and John move out of Newcastle Road to a cottage owned by her husband George in the village of Woolton, just outside of Liverpool and not far from where she lived herself. Of course it also meant that she could see more of her young nephew John. Unable to have children of her own, she had been strongly drawn to John from the moment he was born, and so she welcomed the chance to develop their relationship. The move also gave John, now just two years of age, the opportunity to get to know his Uncle George. Although George Smith and Freddie saw little of each other they were friends, and Freddie felt sure that young John would benefit from his uncle's congenial presence.

Mimi's husband was one of those rare men who was really deserving of the title of 'gentleman'. Not only was he kind and gentle, but his solemn humour and bluff good manners commanded the respect of everyone. In fact he was positively adored by the inhabitants of the village of Woolton, where he was born on his father's dairy farm. Fate, however, dealt him a heavy blow.

His romance with Mimi had started when she was working as a nurse in a hospital in Woolton. Each day, at the time Mimi passed the farm where George, the elder of two sons, was working, he would never fail to be leaning over the gate to pass the time of day with her. This continued – but went no further – for many months, possibly because Mimi was already engaged to a young man who eventually went to work in Kenya, or possibly because George was too afraid to approach her.

Finally, however, George Smith married his pretty nurse, by which time his father had sold his land in Woolton to the company that made 'Bear Brand' silk stockings. On the death of his father, the bulk of the remaining money was bequeathed to George's younger brother, George being left the small amount to be earned from his father's cottage rents. He tried his hand at bookmaking, but was unsuccessful, and finally ended up working in the stocking factory which had been built on his father's land.

The move to Woolton marked the beginning of the rift in the relationship between Julia and Freddie. In the sixteen years that they had been together Julia had never been out on her own in the evenings, despite Freddie's regular absences at sea. But now, free of her parents' influence and living on her own for the first time, during the evenings she began to visit the village pubs which were popular with the forces stationed nearby.

When Freddie had leave and joined her at the cottage he was shocked to discover that she had started drinking, something she had never done before, although she was still unable to down more than one glass of port or sherry without suffering an attack of irrepressible giggles.

'It's not for the drink that I go out,' Julia had tried to reassure him. 'It's the dancing and the singing – it keeps me happy. I've got to do something to cheer myself up while you're away.'

Although he was unhappy about the obvious change in Julia, Freddie thought it best not to make an issue of the matter and decided to join her on the evenings he wasn't fire-watching. Julia was having difficulties in finding a baby-sitter, but Freddie's suggestion of Mimi, who lived conveniently close by, was flatly rejected by Julia.

'Mimi doesn't know that I go out in the evenings and I don't want her to find out. She wouldn't understand and I don't want her lecturing me.' In fact Julia seemed pointedly to avoid meeting Mimi at that time, irritated by her sister's repeated praise of Freddie for the rationed goods such as butter, tea, sugar and soap that he was able to bring home for the two sisters.

The few evenings when Julia and Freddie were able to get out together were no longer much fun. Julia's great love was dancing, but as Freddie couldn't dance he would have to sit and have a drink and a chat with the barman while his wife danced with other men. The other alternative was a movie, but as Julia had worked in a cinema most of her life she could hardly be blamed for not wanting to visit them now. The only other possibility was to stay at home for a laugh and a joke and an early night, which had always been marvellous before but now no longer seemed very exciting to Julia.

The spring of 1943 saw the first-ever row between John's parents. By now Julia was in the habit of visiting the pub in the village every evening and when Freddie, home on leave, suggested they should go out together somewhere else for a change, she reacted with exceptional aggression.

'I'm doing what *I* want now, Freddie, and I want to go down to the village by myself. You've had all these years enjoying yourself and doing what you wanted in life while I've been stuck at home.'

'But now that I'm on leave we can at least get out together, pet. I'll ask Mimi to look after John for a few hours,' said Freddie, heading towards the door.

'No you won't,' countered Julia, actually blocking his path. 'Tonight I'm going out on my own, and as for a baby-sitter it's about time you stayed in and looked after John for a change.'

The conversation was halted by a knock on the door, which Freddie answered in a state of confusion. His bewilderment was increased at the sight of an over-made-up platinum blonde accompanied by her sailor boyfriend.

'Hello, luv,' she began. 'I always call for Julia about this time. Can you see if she's ready yet?'

'Oh, do you? Well, she won't be coming out tonight,' Freddie abruptly informed them, by now feeling angry as well as rather anxious, and to the young woman's astonishment he slammed the door quickly in her face.

It was obvious to Freddie that Julia had changed drastically over the last few months, but he was nevertheless totally unprepared for the violent tirade that followed.

'How dare you speak to my friends like that!' she screamed at him, her face contorted with rage. 'And how dare you decide whether I'm going out or not! I don't bloody well take orders from you!'

As she spoke she had put on her hat and coat and now approached Freddie, who still stood with his back towards the front door, barring her way.

Sensing the seriousness of the situation, he tried to calm his beautiful, red-haired wife. Although she was certainly even more stunning when she was furious, this was a side to her he had never seen before, and he just didn't know how to handle her.

'Please don't go out on your own, darling – not tonight,' he pleaded, stretching out his hands towards her as a propitiatory gesture. But there was obviously to be no appeasing her.

'Are you going to get out of my way or not?' she thundered, folding her arms intransigently, and when Freddie still failed to allow her past him she simply turned on her heel and marched through to the back kitchen where she calmly opened the window, climbed out and ran after her friends to catch them up.

Freddie was asleep by the time Julia returned that evening, so it was not until breakfast the next morning that he had the chance to talk things over with her over a cup of tea. Genuinely perplexed, Freddie was hopeful of discovering the reason for Julia's total change of attitude towards

41

him. But his questions were met by a sullen shrug of the shoulders and a totally untypical silence. Feeling exasperated by a sense of hopelessness, Freddie made one last attempt to elicit some kind of response.

'Your mother would have been ashamed of the way you behaved last night, Julia. She never treated your father that way, whatever the circumstances. She'd be disgusted with you, and you know it.'

The comment was designed to goad his wife – her mother, Anne, had only recently died – and although he was finally successful in evoking a response from Julia it was certainly not along the lines he had expected.

'Keep my mother out of this,' she answered in a cold voice, and gritting her teeth she stood up and calmly poured a cut of hot tea over Freddie's head. Irrational acts of this kind were not out of character for Julia, who had a sadistic and sometimes masochistic streak – a quirk of hers was that she would always rub salt into her wounds when she had cut herself, and actually seemed to enjoy the pain.

Freddie's automatic reaction was to hit out, slapping Julia across the face – the one and only occasion he ever struck her. Almost immediately this brought on a nose bleed, a problem which had plagued her since childhood and which had necessitated several stays in hospital in the past.

Although sore and smarting from the scalding tea as well as from wounded pride, Freddie's concern was for Julia rather than himself as the nose bleed showed no sign of abating. He was worried about her losing so much blood and on impulse he telephoned Mimi. With her nursing experience she would be better able to cope with the situation than he was, and she could also be relied upon to calm Julia and help her to adopt a more reasonable attitude. True to form, Mimi quickly had everything under control soon after her arrival, and whilst she applied cold compresses to Julia's face she extracted the story of the quarrel from the unhappy pair. As usual she spoke sharply to Julia, urging her to be more appreciative of the money and rations which Freddie regularly provided and to be thankful that he was now beginning to get on in the Merchant Navy.

'A lot of women don't see much of their men at the moment, Julia. Remember that you've more to be grateful for than most.'

Although she resented her sister's comments, Julia seemed to settle down again after Mimi's visit, and for the rest of Freddie's shore leave things almost seemed to return to normal. But when the opportunity arose to move back to 9 Newcastle Road, after Pop had gone to stay with relatives, they decided that it might be best to get away from Woolton and the rows which had dogged them ever since they had moved into the cottage there.

Julia's loneliness was nevertheless still a problem, and although it was nice to have the house to themselves it was inevitable that Julia would feel even more isolated while Freddie was away. They discussed the possibility of letting off part of the house until after the war, which would at least provide some company for Julia, and Freddie even suggested that when peace was declared he might try to find a situation ashore. But although she had entreated him for years to give up the sea and settle down, strangely Julia no longer seemed interested.

Fortunately she had a friend around the corner who was willing to baby-sit regularly, which at least meant that she would be able to get out more. Realizing that she desperately needed to let her hair down now and then – and that anyhow there was no way that he could stop her from doing so – Freddie gave his blessing to her outings.

'Go out and enjoy yourself while I'm away, pet,' were his words as he embraced her one warm July day in 1943 before embarking on what was to be a very long voyage. 'We'll have lots of time together once the war is over. It'll be different then, you'll see, darling.' Little did he realize that it was to be eighteen months before they would see each other again, and that by then the situation between them would indeed be very different.

It all started over a lunchtime drink in the Eagle, a pub frequented by the Merchant Navy boys in Liverpool. Freddie now held a head waiter's rating, which naturally was virtually redundant during wartime, and he was having difficulty finding a suitable situation. He was anxious not to lose his rating by accepting a demotion, as this would seriously prejudice his chances of advancement after the war. But eventually, of course, he would be obliged to sail on whichever ship he was ordered.

For this reason his ears pricked up at the words of a Seamen's Union official who sat himself down at the same table. 'Things are looking up for you chaps with ratings,' he commented breezily. 'You're all being sent to New York, travelling as passengers, and being put up in hotels until you can be shipped as chief stewards in the new "liberty" ships the States are throwing out at the rate of two a week.'

Suitably impressed, Freddie reported to the Merchant Navy Pool where he put his name to the necessary documents and was instructed to join the *Berengaria* as a passenger at two o'clock next morning to be transported to New York. He gave his signature eagerly, not for one moment realizing that he was signing for a period of nearly two years, during which time he was to be branded as a deserter, thrown in jail, and arrive back in England without rating or ship.

That evening he and Julia went out to celebrate courtesy of Mimi, who displayed far more enthusiasm than Julia at the news that he had at last reached the dizzy heights of chief steward, and kept telling Julia, 'I knew he would do it!'

There were two to three hundred, mainly sailors, firemen and stewards, who embarked later that night on the *Berengaria*. As the majority were shown to the third-class accommodation, Freddie couldn't help but feel reassured when he was conducted to a first-class cabin. The situation became even more humorous when his personal waiter turned out to be an old shipmate. 'I hope you have a job for me when you come back with your new ship,' he called out as Freddie gaily sauntered down the gangway to the waiting coaches after they docked.

The first surprise occurred as he alighted on 49th Street outside the Van Cortland Hotel, where the scene resembled Liverpool's Lime Street on a Saturday before a home football match. Hordes of slightly inebriated Scousers were weaving around the hotel where they were all to be accommodated. It soon became obvious that there was to be no question of seniority here, and Freddie's anxiety was increased when he learned that no chief stewards had as yet been lodged at the Van Cortland.

Aware that there was very little he could do about the situation, and given that he was likely to remain in New York for about six weeks, Freddie decided to make the best of things; and with his usual appetite for fun he was soon enjoying the delights of night spots such as the Ritz Towers and the Music Box Canteen. Before long he had also organized the boys to stage their own entertainments at Rikers Bar, where he put on a show every weekend he was in New York in return for free drinks.

The third Saturday evening saw Freddie in his finest form and culminated in what turned out to be one of the greatest thrills of his life. As the club began to fill up, Freddie, somewhat under the influence, leaped to his chair and proceeded to enliven the gaiety with his Adolf Hitler act. In response to roars of approval and shouts of 'encore', he followed with a few numbers from Eddie Canter's Broadway show *Whoopee*, but his *pièce de résistance* on this occasion was an impromptu dance which took him to every corner of the room. He gyrated in response to the stirring music, leaping across tables into the hairy arms of the sailors who released him in perfect timing to continue his sylph-like passage around the gaping onlookers, touching a cheek or coyly bewitching them with ardent glances over a non-existent fan.

The finale was greeted with stupendous applause and shouts of 'Broadway for the boy'. When it was announced that they already had an invitation to Jack Dempsey's bar, Freddie was lifted shoulder-high by his mates and, with a crowd of forty to fifty following, they marched singing and shouting towards Broadway and Jack's bar.

Broadway accepted the boisterous throng as only the happy-go-lucky New Yorkers can. By the time they reached Jack Dempsey's bar the crowd had swelled to dangerous proportions and Freddie had visions of some hefty New York cop running them all in for obstruction. As the procession burst through the swing doors, Freddie was deposited in the centre of the Diamond Horseshoe Bar and was toasted all round by the ill-assorted rabble, who were still chanting 'Broadway for the boy'.

Several of the boys had found jobs around the city thanks to the Van Cortland Hotel's housekeeper, who was running a profitable employment agency on the side. So, armed with an introduction card for Macy's, reputedly the biggest department store in the world, Freddie too decided to try his luck. Fortunately the work was easy and not only helped to pass the time until his predicament could be sorted out but also caused him to gain a great affection for the spirit of New York and the New Yorkers. He was even successful in obtaining a social security card, and if circumstances had been different it is likely he would have wished to remain there, as his son John did so many years later.

When the day of embarkation finally arrived, Freddie travelled to Baltimore to await his orders. Although the 'liberty' ships had been practically thrown together in an incredibly short time, they were nevertheless extremely well planned. Apart from the captain's quarters, which were understandably on the bridge, the rest of the crew's quarters were on the main deck amidships, two only to a cabin, and the kitchen was situated in the centre.

When asked to sign the articles Freddie confidently introduced himself as chief steward, but was immediately challenged by a man in civilian clothes standing next to the captain. 'I am the company's chief steward,' he said. 'So unless you have prior orders from the company, I'm afraid you've come to the wrong ship.' There didn't seem to be much that Freddie could do about the situation, so with the captain's promise to report the incident, and in the belief that they would soon be returning to England, he signed as assistant steward.

It soon became clear, however, that the ship was to carry out a number of trips transporting arms and ammunition between New York and the Far East, and that it would be some time before Freddie would be able to register his complaint. Furious at the trick the Merchant Navy Pool and the Seamen's Union had played upon him, he questioned the captain on the possibility of signing off when the ship docked in New York.

'I'm afraid it's not on, Lennie,' was his reply. 'My instructions are that no one can sign off the ship except by doctor's orders. But if you're determined to register a complaint, your only chance is to miss the ship and report to the consul as soon as the ship has sailed. Mind you, you're a bloody fool if you do – it could land you in it.'

But to Freddie it was the only feasible course of action if he were to retain his rating. He spent the first night ashore lying low, but next morning reported promptly to the British consul, confident that he would arrange for him to join a ship returning to England.

What happened next was a shock, and marked the start of a twelve-month nightmare. After Freddie announced his name at the desk, the young clerk in charge bent down and pressed a button, whereupon two tall uniformed men appeared from an office behind, flanked him on either side and snapped 'We're immigration officers, you'd better come with us. You're under suspicion of desertion.'

They took him to Ellis Island, where he spent two miserable weeks before discovering what was to happen to him. His first concern was Julia and the baby, as he was aware that she would not receive any wages while he was in this mess, and so he asked the consulate to ensure that word would reach her about his predicament. As he had constantly instructed her to report to the Seamen's Union to request assistance should such a situation ever arise, he felt sure that she would receive help.

But back home in Liverpool, Christmas was approaching and Julia had received no news of her man for months. None of Freddie's letters at this time had reached her, and neither had the consulate passed on any information as to what had become of him.

Having recently celebrated his third birthday, John was just beginning to become aware of what Christmas was all about, and was especially excited at the prospect of a visit from Father Christmas. He was also very hopeful that his father might be home for the festivities, and repeatedly pestered his mother as to when Daddy would be back from the war.

For Julia the situation was a difficult one. Her worst problem was lack of funds, since Freddie's wages had stopped and she had received no assistance from the Seamen's Union. There was no alternative but to swallow her pride and accept the generosity of the Stanley family, or there would be no presents for young John that Christmas.

Worse, the absence of letters, so unusual for Freddie, had aroused her fears as to his safety. And although she attempted to cheer up young John by giving him a ship's concert programme which billed his Daddy as singing 'Begin the Beguine', and which Freddie had enclosed for

48

the boy in his last letter, she did confide to Mimi that she was afraid she might never see Freddie again.

She was already in the habit of going dancing in the evenings with her friends and had built up a happy and flourishing social life. But whereas until now she had restricted herself to one-night stands – of a strictly platonic nature, with the sudden uncertainty about her husband she now allowed herself to take a little more interest in her dancing partners.

Like so many young people parted from their loved ones by the war, she had no way of knowing what the future held for Freddie or for herself. There was really very little alternative but to live each day for itself, regardless of the consequences. And after all, the last letter she had received from Freddie before his mysterious disappearance had concluded with these words: 'I realize how difficult it must be for you while I'm away, and particularly during long periods, but I beg of you don't sit around the fire moping. Get out and enjoy yourself, for we none of us know when this war will end or how.'

Early in February Freddie received a letter from the consul, ordering him to join a ship named the *Sammex*, bound for the Far East, under threat of being charged with desertion. But his troubles were still far from over.

The *Sammex* had not been more than a week at sea before Freddie's suspicions were aroused regarding the cargo. It wasn't necessary to be a detective to realize that there was an unusually large amount of whisky, cigarettes and beer on board that was certainly far in excess of crew issue.

Therefore he was hardly surprised when the second cook, a likeable young Cockney, offered him a bottle of Johnny Walker with the cryptic comment, 'There's plenty more where that came from.'

'I presume this is broached cargo?' asked Freddie, examining the bottle.

'Yes,' was the smiling reply. 'The stevedores and bo'sun in New York and all the crew are in on it – apart from the wireless operator and the captain, of course.

'Well, it's very kind of you,' remarked Freddie, anxious to avoid any further trouble. 'But don't implicate me in this. I want to keep my hands clean.'

The rest of the voyage continued with the crew trying their utmost to dispense with the loot in an orgy of drinking and smoking. In fact such was the revelry that 'Sparks', the wireless operator, became suspicious and wired the authorities in Bône, North Africa. As soon as they had dropped anchor in the bay they were boarded by the military police.

While the search was in progress Freddie was sitting in his cabin where his mate, 'Limey', had just opened a bottle of ice-cold beer and poured out two glasses. 'I'll be back in a minute, Lennie,' he called, as he went out to collect some cigarettes.

Freddie had barely sipped from the glass when a voice from the doorway remarked, 'Good health, sailor. Is this your cabin?' Turning, he saw two Redcaps who now approached him. 'Could we have a look at the bottle?' one said, picking it up without waiting for a reply. 'This is not ship's issue,' he announced, passing the bottle to his colleague.

'Of course it is,' Freddie replied, knowing full well that it wasn't, but not anticipating the drastic results.

'You'd better come along with us,' was the sharp retort.

On landing ashore Freddie was pushed into an army jeep, escorted by Redcaps as if he were Al Capone himself, and amidst a hail of jibes and shrieks from the Arab loiterers was whisked away through Bône along a winding road that led halfway up a mountain to the naval barracks.

Later that day, together with several other members of the crew who were also under arrest, he was marched through the town to the court room with a guard of six matelots. Again they were followed by an ever-swelling mob of Arabs, hissing, spitting and throwing stones, who pushed their way into the court room, no doubt hopeful of a morning's free entertainment.

The charge was that of stealing by finding, and the sentence – at the insistence of the overweight British consul in Malta, who presided over the court – was three months' detainment at the army prison. Despite his sense of outrage Freddie did have the consolation of knowing that it would be some weeks before he would actually be sent to the jail on the hill, since documents had to be sent to Malta for verification. In fact he had only nine days of his sentence left to serve when they eventually took him up the hill, and, resilient as he was to hardship, he affirmed that any more than nine days in that hell-hole would certainly have left its mark.

The majority of the inmates were Eighth Army boys who had been detained for refusing to move another inch until 'Monty' fulfilled some of the many promises he had made to the troops as a reward for their heroic efforts in pushing Rommel across North Africa. The conditions in the jail and the treatment of the prisoners by the screws were so disgusting as to be indescribable, and Freddie himself was set the loathsome task of cleaning the squalid lavatories. But on his release he was left in no doubt that the horror of the establishment was to be kept hushed up.

'The moment you walk through that gate,' thundered the unrelenting commandant, 'You will forget everything you have seen or heard in this prison. If you choose to ignore my warning, there are places other than prisons where people like you can be confined without trial.' And Freddie was under no illusion as to what he meant.

It was four-thirty in the afternoon when he began the long trek down the hill towards the town, penniless, weak and hungry. Having received no directions as to the quickest route, it was early evening before he found his bearings, by which time dusk was descending.

51

The path to the town led through the dreaded Casbah, a mass of dark and narrow alleys, which white men entered at peril of being attacked by Arabs, either with stones or with a long bamboo rod with a razor blade or sharp knife attached to the end. Frequently the Arabs beat their victims unconscious and stripped them naked, leaving them to find their own way out.

By the time Freddie reached the Casbah the sky was pitch-black and he could see nothing at all on either side of him. Beset with panic by stories he had heard from other sailors, he immediately began to run as fast as he possibly could, but despite his speed he felt the impact of stones hitting him from all sides, thrown by unseen hands.

As always when in dire straits he thought of Polly, his beloved mother, and perhaps it was she who directed his feet in the right direction. Certainly, the few lights of Bône were the most joyful sight he had ever beheld as he staggered cut and bleeding into the arms of a huge man wearing a leather jacket and jeans.

His name was Hans, a Dutchman working for the underground, whose offer of help Freddie gratefully accepted and to whom he poured out the whole of his sad story.

'And if I could get my hands on that bloody consul!' he concluded.

'He's in there,' remarked Hans calmly, pointing to the office behind them. 'I'll help you sort him out. You go in and see him and I'll attend to his secretary.'

Bleeding and dishevelled, Freddie pushed his way into the consul's private office yelling, 'Look at me, you fat bastard! This is all your bloody fault!'

'What do you want?' asked the consul coldly.

'Money, you bloody fool,' a voice said from the door through which Hans had entered, dragging the terrified secretary with him.

'My God, not you,' the startled consul gasped, and it was

52

obvious that he not only knew Hans but was also afraid of him.

'I'll give you five minutes to have a nice chat,' said Hans and dragged the secretary out again.

'Here's five dollars for now,' said the consul, hurriedly opening a drawer of the desk. 'And you can get some new clothes from the hostel.'

Suddenly all Freddie's pent-up fury erupted at this degrading suggestion, as he looked at the overweight, overdressed representative of so-called British justice. He hit him hard and square between the eyes, then ran around his desk and gave him a few more for his mates.

'Now hand over fifty dollars before I send for the Dutchman,' he warned him. The money was duly passed over without a word.

Freddie hadn't felt better for months, and with Hans's reassurance that the consul wouldn't dare report the episode he went with him to the hotel he was staying at and booked a room.

It was some weeks before he was successful in finding a place on the *Monarch of Bermuda*, now serving as a troopship, which was to transport him back to England as a DBS (Distressed British Seaman). All he now possessed were the clothes he stood up in, his wallet containing a few American dollars and his US social security card, which he discovered too late would have entitled him to help from the American consul.

Whilst queuing to change his few dollars into English currency, he was approached by a friendly young steward by the name of Billy Hall.

'How much are you changing?' the man enquired.

'Oh, just a few bucks,' he replied.

'Change fifty for me,' he asked, and so a long friendship began.

When they arrived back in Liverpool it was a cold and foggy

November evening in 1944. As he said his goodbyes to Billy Hall, promising to call on him some time in Blackpool where he lived, Freddie suddenly became aware that he was virtually destitute.

He realized, of course, that he couldn't go home as he was, after nearly eighteen months away, and he felt at a loss as to what to do as he strolled up and down the Pier Head, pondering the situation.

Looking at the old, familiar sight of the Liver Building clock pointing to five-thirty he decided to phone Sydney, who was still at the shop and who agreed to meet him at six o'clock. Had Freddie not greeted his brother with a 'Hello, Syd,' he would almost certainly have passed him by, for he had lost a lot of weight since they had last met.

'By the look of you,' snorted Sydney, 'it's not just clothes you need.'

'I feel great,' Freddie answered cheerfully.

'You're as thin as a rake. Your wife won't recognize you – that is, if she lets you back home,' he announced ominously.

As ever, reliable Sydney came to the rescue and fixed up Freddie with a suit, an overcoat and a suitcase containing a shirt and underclothes and some toilet requisites, and over a drink in the Big House Freddie recounted as much as he could of his adventures. Half an hour later saw him much restored in body and soul and, in light-hearted mood, he hailed a taxi for 9 Newcastle Road.

3
LITTLE PAL

As Freddie gave the familiar knocker a sharp rap, his mind turned to Sydney's jibing comment that Julia might not let him home. It was certainly true that eighteen months had passed since he was last in Liverpool, and it was inevitable that the situation at home must have changed. It was not so much his family's financial plight that concerned him, as he was sure that Julia would have been supplied with funds by the Union. He just had a nagging fear that they might no longer know how to talk to each other.

And what of his reception by little John? The boy had been just two and a half when he had last sailed away, far too young to have formed any firm memories of his Daddy. Now he had just celebrated his fourth birthday. Would he greet his father as a total stranger?

Freddie's thoughts were interrupted when the door was abruptly opened by a small, middle-aged woman whom he did not recognize.

'Yes?' she enquired.

'I live here,' said Freddie hesitantly.

'Oh.' Her alarm was most puzzling to him. 'You must be Mr Lennon, then,' and, visibly pulling herself together, she invited him in. 'Your wife's out,' she said, 'but the boy's in bed.'

'That's nice,' he said, more puzzled than ever. 'I suppose you're baby-sitting for her?'

'Oh, no,' she replied quite vehemently. 'I live here. My husband and I have the downstairs rooms.' And with this she took him into her sitting room.

As Freddie sat down, bewildered, the woman suggested a pot of tea and went out to the kitchen to make it. He remembered of course that he and Julia had discussed taking in lodgers to help out financially, but he felt very disorientated, especially by Julia's absence.

The lodger returned with the tea and carefully poured out two cups. She had now recovered her composure and sat down opposite Freddie with the obvious intention of finding out all she could about him, and also filling him in on what had been happening at home while he was away.

'Julia won't be home before twelve o'clock,' she began. 'She goes dancing nearly every night.'

'I'm well aware of all that,' replied Freddie coldly. 'I did write to her and suggest that she should go out a little.'

'Oh, I only thought I'd better prepare you for it,' said the woman, a little peeved. 'She might bring her boyfriend home for supper.'

While Freddie was considering this disturbing news the lodger left him to take a cup of tea to her husband, and when she returned she handed him a piece of paper with a name, rank and camp of a private soldier. 'You might need this,' she added knowingly.

To Freddie this was far from cheering news after his ordeals of the last eighteen months, but he certainly didn't blame Julia for enjoying a social life while he was away. After all, even if she had received word of his imprisonment she had no way of knowing whether she would ever see him again. But supposing she had found someone else in his absence? She was still as attractive as ever, and had never been short of admirers.

All these worries raced through his mind as he waited in the upstairs flat for Julia to come home. Eventually, at about eleven-thirty, he heard the key click in the lock and Julia's step on the stairs. At the same time the lodger, who no doubt was also listening for her return, opened the door and loudly proclaimed, 'Your husband's come home.'

'Hello,' Julia greeted him, deliberately averting her eyes from his. 'I'm pregnant.'

It was probably the months of disillusionment that kept Freddie in his chair. 'That's rather a sick joke after all this time,' he replied feebly.

'It's no joke,' she responded as she took off her coat and defiantly threw back her long red hair.

'This is great news to greet me with. Why on earth did you have to fire it at me like this?'

'You're a good one to talk,' she returned. 'Where the hell have you been for the last eighteen months? We've had no word, no money – we all thought you were dead.'

'Well, I'm alive and kicking, and after all these months of dreaming of seeing you again this is a bloody awful homecoming.'

'You had to know the truth,' she blurted out, taking a seat. 'I've been seeing a man while you were away, and one evening he lost control of himself and raped me.'

'I'll bloody well kill him!' was Freddie's indignant reply.

'No, you won't, because it wasn't entirely his fault. I was just as much to blame. Anyway, it's happened and there's nothing that you, I or anyone can do about it.' And with a shrug of her shoulders she lit a cigarette.

The extraordinary thing about the whole business was that it had occurred only a few weeks before Freddie's return, and Julia had only discovered a few days earlier that she was in fact pregnant.

Freddie was anxious to find out the full facts, but Julia would divulge nothing and refused even to name the man concerned. However, he did have the piece of paper given to him by the lodger with the details of the soldier who had been referred to as Julia's boyfriend. So the next day, armed with the piece of paper and accompanied by his devoted younger brother Charlie, he set out to get to the bottom of the matter.

The army private was billeted in a camp on the other side

of the Mersey in Cheshire. When they arrived Freddie asked to see the officer in charge and stated his business to him in confidence. The officer was very helpful and agreed to arrange for the soldier to have compassionate leave, should it prove necessary.

The young soldier was summoned and he and Freddie were shown into a small interview room where they could have a quiet conversation. He was a tall, blond, good-looking Welsh boy by the name of Williams, and in spite of himself Freddie found him extremely likeable on first meeting.

'I'm Julia's husband,' began Freddie, to which the Welsh boy appeared to apologize for himself, explaining that he was serious about Julia and loved her.

'I met her about six months ago at a dance,' he confided. 'And all along I've been absolutely crazy about her.'

'And what of her feelings for you?' Freddie wanted to know.

'That's the problem,' Williams went on. 'I don't think she feels the same way about me. She always says that it's you she loves, and that she was waiting for you regardless of what had happened to you.'

'But now she's carrying your child,' said Freddie, looking him squarely in the eye. 'What the hell are we going to do about it?'

'I want to marry her,' Williams replied eagerly. 'That is, if you'll divorce her.'

'Well, in that case I think you'd better come home with us and we'll discuss it all together,' said Freddie, and that is precisely what they did.

Julia appeared amazed at the sight of the three men on the doorstep.

'Your boyfriend claims he wants to marry you. What do you say?' were Freddie's first words as they all trooped into the lounge.

'Yes, Julia, you know I love you and I'll stick by you,'

Williams added quickly.

Julia's reaction was an outburst of derisive laughter. 'I don't want you, you bloody fool,' she said, turning her back on him.

The young Welsh boy's face fell, and Freddie honestly felt sorry for him. Charlie, with his usual rough diplomacy, went into the kitchen to make a cup of tea.

When Freddie invited the soldier to sit down, Julia angrily demanded to know how he had found him.

'That's my business,' replied Freddie shortly. 'The question is what we are going to do about the baby. He says he wants to marry you.'

'Well, I don't want to marry him and that's final,' she replied, and turning to the deflated young Welshman she said, 'Drink your tea and get lost.'

Freddie and Charlie accompanied the soldier out and took him for a drink to get over the shock. It seemed that his parents were comfortably off and owned a farm in Wales, and his parting comment before he returned to the camp was that he was sure they would be happy to adopt the baby.

When Freddie arrived back at Newcastle Road he found that Mimi had called, having heard that Freddie had at last arrived home. She was naturally astonished when Julia coolly announced she was pregnant, but surprise soon gave way to anger and she gave Julia a severe tongue lashing whilst her sister listened, bored and half smiling.

Mimi's main worry was the scandal, so when Freddie assured her that he would stand by his wife, Mimi hugged him with delight and repeatedly told Julia what a wonderful husband she had.

But when Pop Stanley heard the news his sense of outrage was not so easily appeased, and for the first time in his life, his natural affection for Julia was overcome by a sense of shame. To the amazement of all concerned, he issued his favourite daughter with a cruel ultimatum.

'The baby must be adopted or you will leave this house

and no longer consider yourself a daughter of mine.'

The logical solution appeared to be that Mimi should adopt the baby – at forty-two she was still childless – but she was not keen to take on an illegitimate child, and in any case Pop Stanley firmly forbade any of the family to become involved with it. Julia refused to have anything to do with Williams, the father of her child, who might have been able to take the baby. So the only remaining answer was that the baby should be adopted via an agency, and here Mimi was the perfect accessory. With her nursing experience and her contacts in the profession she was able to make the necessary arrangements for the adoption of the child and took matters firmly in her capable hands.

Little John had grown up a lot in the eighteen months since Freddie had last seen him and was already starting to show signs of perceptive intelligence. As it was approaching Christmas, Freddie took the opportunity to take John round all the big Liverpool stores to buy presents, but despite his delight he was extremely puzzled to find a Santa Claus in every store they visited. 'Just how many Father Christmases are there?' he wanted to know.

For father and son it was a good opportunity to get to know each other – once a major hurdle had been overcome.

'Do I have to call you Pater, Daddy? Aunt Mimi says I must because that's what my cousin Stanley calls his father,' remarked John loudly one day on the bus.

'I'd much sooner you didn't,' was Freddie's somewhat embarrassed reply, as a curious hush fell among the passengers. It's rather unusual for Scousers to call their father 'Pater'!

The next few weeks were spent exploring the city and watching the big ships from the Pier Head.

'One day we'll go on a long voyage together, won't we, Daddy?' John would smile.

'I just wish I could take you with me, son,' was Freddie's

regretful reply.

The days passed happily, but having just got to know each other it was particularly disappointing when Freddie received orders from the Pool to proceed to Southampton to join the *Dominion Monarch* only three days before Christmas.

The months that followed were a very puzzling period for John. As Julia's pregnancy advanced steadily, she found it difficult to answer John's probing questions. Now that it had been settled that her child was to be adopted she was uncertain how she would explain to John why the baby would not be coming home.

Mimi had arranged for Julia's confinement to take place at Elmswood, a Salvation Army hostel in North Mossley Hill Road, and it was here that she gave birth to a beautful little girl on 19 June 1945. Julia's parting gift to her child was to name her Victoria Elizabeth – the only influence she would ever have over her daughter's life. But it was not until the arrangements for the adoption were finally settled that she realized the enormity of her loss. The tragedy was to mark a change in her personality, and the carefree frivolity of her youth was over forever.

Freddie too had thought of little else except the baby for some time, and when he visited Julia at the hostel he tried to convince her to keep the baby if she so wished, regardless of Pop Stanley's opposition, and suggested that it should be brought up as their own child. But it seemed that her father's wishes were of paramount importance, for she was resolute in her refusal and actually forbade Freddie to mention the subject again.

The policy at Elmswood was that the natural parents and the adoptive parents should know as little as possible about one another, and the only information that Freddie could obtain from the matron was that the baby had gone to a good home. 'A sailor like yourself,' she said. 'A Norwegian captain and his wife.'

61

Later, when he looked back on his visits to Julia at the hostel, Freddie could hardly believe that it had all been so nice and friendly. Despite the heaviness of her heart, Julia did not betray to Freddie the hurt she was feeling. She kept her sorrow to herself, as she had been accustomed to throughout their relationship.

They laughed and joked together just as they had done in the old days, and Freddie really believed that she was looking forward to coming home and resuming where they had left off before the war. He returned to the ship under the impression that everything was all right and he was hopeful that by the end of his next trip things would begin to return to normal for him once more.

As Freddie walked towards the house on a dark evening in March 1946, he caught sight of Julia standing in the street talking to a man. He knew that she had recognized him, so he hurried on expecting to be let in by the lodger, but it was George Stanley who answered his knock.

'Hello,' he said. 'Julia's gone out for a few minutes.'

'I know,' replied Freddie. 'I've just seen her talking to some fellow.' Pop Stanley did not reply but walked out into the street. He returned a few minutes later with Julia and the man, who was duly introduced to Freddie as a Bobby Dykins, who like himself worked in the catering trade. From the awkward silence Freddie soon sensed there was something seriously wrong. That George Stanley and Bobby Dykins were acquainted was obvious, and the fact that the lodgers were missing was also rather mystifying.

Freddie opened the conversation by asking why the lodgers had left.

'I've come back to live here, so we don't need them,' said Pop Stanley, and then to Freddie's astonishment he went on: 'Anyway, it's my house.'

'The rent book is in my name,' retorted Freddie hotly.

'Not any more. Mimi had it changed back to mine,' was

62

Pop's triumphant rejoinder as he flourished the book under his son-in-law's nose. Sure enough, Freddie's name had been crossed out and George Stanley's written in above it. Seemingly, all the old animosity between them had been rekindled.

'I'll see the landlord about that,' Freddie told him, and turning to Julia, who was standing to one side white and silent, he asked her none too politely, 'What the hell do you know about this?'

'That's why I'm here,' intervened her father. 'To protect her.'

'To protect her from what?' yelled Freddie, whereupon Bobby, as yet silent, hesitantly chipped in, 'I know you've struck her.'

'I don't know who you are,' breathed Freddie, feeling the wrath rise within him, 'but you'd better get out and damned quickly.' All at once the frustrated rage which Freddie had so far kept successfully under control demanded immediate release and he grabbed his rival by the collar, addressing him in a torrent of abuse.

On his guard, due to Pop Stanley's exaggerated tales of Freddie's volatile temperament, Dykins made as if to defend himself, and for a moment it appeared that a fight was likely to break out. George Stanley himself soon joined in the affray, thundering out his orders to his daughter's angry lovers.

But it was his mother's screams that finally awoke young John, who listened terrified from the top of the stairs, not understanding but knowing that something was very wrong. He recognized his father's voice but he had never heard him shouting this way before. He longed to protect his mother, to calm her screams, but he felt powerless to stop things.

To John the argument seemed to continue for hours, but in reality it was only after a few minutes that Freddie finally propelled Bobby Dykins to the front door and told him in sailor's language to clear off.

63

When Freddie went back into the house he found Julia and her father in close conference, whispering quietly together.

'I only ever hit you once. Tell your father why,' said Freddie, turning to Julia.

She did not answer, but George Stanley interrupted to say, 'I'm not leaving you two alone tonight'. He sat down determinedly and folded his arms.

'You can stay,' replied Freddie, 'but only because of your age. Tomorrow you can get out and take the rent book back to Mimi.'

Julia and Freddie sat up for hours discussing the situation. Although Freddie had believed that things had returned to normal between them, as far as Julia was concerned their relationship had not been the same since the birth of Victoria Elizabeth. For although Freddie had 'forgiven' her, she felt that he looked down on her, and his own unerring faithfulness was an irritating reminder of her mistake.

Julia had met Bobby Dykins some six months previously, shortly after recovering from her confinement. He had been kind to her and had cheered her up, helping her to put the past behind her.

'For the last year you've been away for three or four months at a time,' explained Julia. 'You just weren't around when I needed you, but he was.'

'But surely you don't intend to break up our marriage after all the years we've been together,' remonstrated Freddie, beginning to pace up and down the lounge.

'That's just what I do intend to do,' she replied. 'Our marriage has been over for a long time now, ever since I got myself pregnant.'

'Look, you know I would have adopted the baby – I thought we'd put that behind us. There's never been another girl for me except you, Julia, in all these years.'

'Well, in that case it seems you're just too good for me,'

she commented with a hint of sarcasm in her voice. 'We're through, Freddie, and I'm leaving you tomorrow.'

Despite the seriousness of the conversation Freddie just couldn't believe that it was over between them when later, just as they had always done, they made passionate love.

'No one makes love like you,' murmured Julia as she turned out the light – a dubious compliment, he felt, implying that she was sufficiently experienced to judge his sexual performance. But he pushed the doubts from his mind and still felt certain that she would be in a different frame of mind next morning.

But it was not to be. At about ten o'clock he was awoken by Julia with a cup of tea and the news that her father had left, taking John with him. Feeling extremely anxious, he hurried downstairs where a woman who was vaguely familiar was helping Julia to move the furniture out of the house.

'You will at least leave me a chair, won't you?' asked Freddie light-heartedly, but it was evident from Julia's uncompromising expression that this time she was not joking. The neighbour, who was taking Julia's furniture into her own house for the time being, diplomatically decided to leave them alone.

'You don't really mean to go, do you, pet?' asked Freddie quietly.

'Yes, I do.'

'But what about John? Stay for his sake, if not for your own.'

'What difference will it make to him? He hardly sees anything of you anyway. The sea has always been more important to you than we have. If you hadn't been so obsessed with losing your rating you'd never have jumped ship in New York, which was when everything started to go wrong between us. You can't just disappear for eighteen months and expect things to be the same. You made your decision, and now I've made mine.' And with these words

Julia walked out of the house through the back door and called to her friend to return.

Somehow things seemed so final that to his bewilderment Freddie found himself helping them out with the furniture, and before twelve o'clock everything had gone except for one broken chair which was left for him to sit on, exactly as he had requested. Yet against all reason his hopes were still alive that she would eventually change her mind.

'When you're ready to come back you can contact me through Sydney,' he said, handing his brother's phone number to Julia as she was about to leave. But it was a one-sided conversation, and neither did she answer when Freddie asked whether her father had taken John to Mimi's.

He couldn't of course remain in an empty house, but he did stay on in Liverpool for about two weeks, risking expulsion from the Pool for refusing vacancies, in the expectation that Julia would contact him. Finally, having heard no word, it was with a heavy heart that he accepted Sydney's advice and visited a solicitor, who had the usual paragraph inserted in the papers stating that he would not be responsible for debts incurred by his wife and so on. An opportunity arose to join the *Queen Mary* as a night steward; reluctantly he accepted, and once again took the train to Southampton.

It was less than an hour before the ship was due to sail that a messenger came aboard from the dock office to inform Freddie that a phone call had been taken for him from a Mrs Smith of Menlove Avenue, instructing him to visit her immediately. As Mimi had given no reason why she needed to see him, Freddie was unable to gain permission from the chief steward to 'break articles' and leave the ship, but he was allowed to go ashore in order to make a phone call.

Mimi's frantic appeal was that John was unhappy and badly needed looking after. She claimed that Julia wasn't caring for him properly and that he had walked by himself from Newcastle Road all the way to her house in Woolton, where she was now looking after him. At Freddie's request Mimi brought John to the phone.

'Hello, John,' began Freddie, trying his best to sound bright and cheerful.

'Hello, Daddy. When are you coming home?' asked the confused little boy, at which Freddie felt rather helpless, knowing that it would be a fortnight at the earliest before he could be back in Liverpool.

For John the past few weeks had been both traumatic and confusing. Shortly after Freddie's departure from Newcastle Road, Julia had reinstalled her furniture and had moved back into No. 9 with Bobby Dykins – much to the disgust of Pop Stanley, who disapproved strongly of their 'immoral behaviour'. Completely disorientated by this sudden turn of events, John found himself confronted with a new father, a situation which his sensitive young mind was quite unable to accept.

'I don't like my new Daddy,' continued John. 'When will you be coming back for me?'

'I'll be home in two weeks, John,' was Freddie's attempt at a reassuring reply. 'In the meantime I want you to stay with your Auntie Mimi, and remember I'll be there just as soon as I can.'

The next two weeks were a worrying time. Despite the fun of visiting the Capital on Broadway when the ship docked in New York, to see a new singer named Frank Sinatra who was just beginning to make a name for himself, Freddie's thoughts were constantly preoccupied with John and what was to be done on his return.

On disembarking in Southampton he immediately caught the train for Liverpool. It was about seven in the evening by the time he arrived at Mimi's house in Menlove Avenue. John had already been put to bed and Mimi thought it better not to disturb him as he would be able to see his Daddy in the morning.

She went into the kitchen to make some tea, but before the kettle had boiled she had presented Freddie with a list of expenses incurred since John's arrival at her home, a gesture which both surprised and horrified her brother-in-law. Although in the past he had always been fond of Mimi – despite the obsession with propriety which she shared with his brother Sydney – he now gained the impression that she was becoming over-concerned about the financial aspects of the affair. And although he said nothing at the time, he made up his mind at that instant that the only course of action would be to take John away with him.

Mimi shared her father's disapproval of Julia's behaviour and informed Freddie in horrified tones that she had actually moved back into Newcastle Road with her boy-friend with whom she was now 'living in sin'. Saddened by this news and exasperated by Mimi's lecture on Julia's misdoings, Freddie finally went up to bed feigning tired-ness, but not before he had given Mimi £20 to cover her expenses over the last couple of weeks.

He slept fitfully that night, debating with himself what to do. There hadn't been any talk of divorce, which he might have agreed to, but he certainly hadn't any intention of starting proceedings himself. Mimi had claimed that Julia was neglecting John, but the fact that she hadn't shown any interest in adopting Julia's other baby, and the immediate demand for money that very evening, convinced Freddie that it would be better not to leave John with his sister-in-law. He finally made up his mind that he would take John to stay with his friend Billy Hall at the seaside resort of Blackpool, making some excuse to Mimi that he was taking John out shopping or to see his Granny.

He was awakened the following morning by a very excited young John dancing and shouting and jumping on the bed, overjoyed to see his Daddy again. He was soon joined by his cousin Leila, Harriet's daughter, who was more or less the same age as himself. Leila was staying with Mimi to keep

John company, and now she began to try to pull the sheets off the bed until Mimi screamed, 'Come downstairs at once, Leila, until your uncle gets dressed!' It was then that Freddie asked John whether he would like to go out with him for the day.

'Oh yes, Daddy, just us two,' said John, hugging his father with glee, and he careered downstairs, yelling to Mimi over and over again, 'Daddy's taking me out today.'

Over breakfast, Mimi appeared to be in full agreement with Freddie's suggestion that he should take John out; but she hinted that she would prefer to accompany them by remarking that John needed more clothes and that Freddie wouldn't be much use in choosing them. But, as fate had it, Mimi was already committed to taking Leila back home that morning, which meant that John would after all have his Daddy to himself. And before Mimi was even out of sight, Freddie was heading for the tram stop with John gaily tripping at his side.

They arrived at Billy Hall's home in Blackpool about midday, ill prepared for a long stay but glad to be together at last. Billy and his brother were out on business, but they received an overwhelming welcome from his Mum and Dad who hugged and kissed John, much to his embarrassment, as though he were one of their own.

Mr and Mrs Hall were a typical Lancashire-bred home-loving couple and possessed the qualities which endear Lancastrians to those who have enjoyed their hospitality. Mrs Hall was a small, sweet, happy-looking woman who took great pride in her lovely little home, while her husband was a slow-moving, amiable man who worked at the local greyhound stadium and knew every dog by name.

The first week was one of joy for John and his Daddy, and Freddie doubted whether he had ever seen the lad so happy. There hardly seemed to be enough hours in the day for John to fit in all the things he longed to do with his new-found father, and although Mr and Mrs Hall were early risers,

69

John's insistence that they should all get up about seven o'clock in the morning was a bit too much. Such was his enthusiasm that, if he couldn't drag Freddie out himself, he coaxed Mrs Hall to put on Daddy's favourite record – Joan Hammond singing 'One Fine Day'. Much as Freddie loved the song, the noise finally forced him out of his bed to tend to John's wishes, generally a visit to the fair or a run on the beach. Indeed, this procedure became a ritual – little wonder that John didn't care for the classics!

It was during one of these early morning strolls on the seashore that a terrifying incident occurred which remained impressed upon John's subconscious for many years to come. It was a cheerless morning and the beach was almost deserted except for large numbers of screeching seagulls which were soaring powerfully across the water. John was running on ahead of Freddie, enjoying the pure salty air and the exhilarating sense of freedom. Freddie was smoking, and while his gaze was diverted for a moment as he lit another cigarette the little boy tumbled into a deep gully of sand and disappeared from view.

Struck by fear at John's sudden disappearance, Freddie ran anxiously up and down the beach scanning the horizon for some glimpse of the little lad, but he was nowhere to be seen. As his sense of panic mounted, Freddie began shouting John's name over and over again, cupping his mouth with his hands in a vain attempt to be heard above the cacophony of the seabirds.

It seemed like an age, but it was in fact a full five minutes before, having ceased his useless calling in order to listen for John's voice, Freddie finally heard faint screams of 'Daddy, Daddy,' which directed him to where John lay – fortunately unhurt, but very frightened.

Freddie had been careful to keep his new address strictly secret, the only member of his family who was aware of his whereabouts being his elder brother Sydney. And it was to Sydney that John was now despatched while Freddie spent a couple of weeks in Southampton helping Billy Hall with his black market business in nylons.

The move came as an unwelcome shock to young John, and only further increased his feelings of insecurity. But to Sydney and his wife Madge the visit was a delightful opportunity to get to know their young nephew, whom they had hardly met since he was born. Like Mimi and George Smith, they too were childless and were anxious to seize the opportunity to adopt John and bring him up as the son they had always longed for. Sydney managed to convince Freddie that he would be unlikely to be granted custody of the child with a profession such as his, and although no definite agreement was made that they should adopt the child, by the time John returned with Freddie to Blackpool Sydney and his wife were under the impression that they were to be granted the guardianship of their nephew.

Back in Blackpool the carefree outings resumed for several more weeks, but cash was fast running out and Freddie knew that he would soon have to go back to sea again. Billy Hall's advice was to find a ship sailing to 'Aussie' and New Zealand.

'Mum and Dad are emigrating to New Zealand now that I have enough money to open a business there,' he told Freddie. 'They're knocked out by your John and think it would be a good idea if they took him with them and we could join them over there as soon as they are settled.' By this he meant that they could take stewards' jobs on a ship sailing to New Zealand and leave it on arrival, a practice very much in vogue at that time until it became abused out of all proportion and ships were returning home undermanned. The Halls now joined Mimi Smith and Sydney Lennon as prospective adoptive parents: the guardianship of the young John Lennon was indeed hotly contested.

On reflection Freddie was inclined to think that emigration might be the answer to his problem – although it would mean a disappointment for Sydney and his wife – and as

71

John seemed to be thrilled at the prospect of going on a long voyage just like Daddy, he made up his mind to put the plan into action. Fate, however, decreed otherwise.

On Saturday, 22 June 1946 Freddie was in the process of finalizing arrangements for John to travel to New Zealand with the Halls when the last person in the world he had expected to see again appeared at the door. It was Julia, accompanied by her boyfriend Bobby Dykins, who hovered nervously at the gate whilst she announced herself to Mrs Hall.

'How the hell did you find out where I was living?' demanded Freddie, coming to the door.

'We enquired at the Pool Office,' she replied, hardly looking at him, and the meekness of her manner was so unfamiliar that it caused Freddie to look at her more closely. She had always been very meticulous with regard to clothes, but the ill-shaped costume she was wearing, which made her look positively matronly, was definitely out of character with the girl Freddie knew or the wicked person Mimi had pictured for him.

'What for?' asked Freddie.

'I want to take John back,' she replied.

Evidently it was to be a long conversation, so he called to Mrs Hall to take John into the kitchen and then asked Julia to come in.

'I'm not letting you take him back to Mimi,' resumed Freddie as she sat down.

'Oh, no,' said Julia, and then launched into a lengthy explanation that she had obtained a new home – a flat in Gateacre – where she was settling down with Bobby and wanted John back with her.

'You know that you wouldn't be able to give him a proper home while you're away at sea,' she went on.

Freddie was apprehensive that Julia would oppose his idea of taking John to New Zealand, but to his surprise she made no objections when he told her of his plan.

'You must love him, then,' was all she said, moving towards the door with her eyes cast down. Then, on impulse, she asked, 'Can I see him before I go?' Freddie called to Mrs Hall to bring John into the lounge.

'Hello, Mummy,' he said a little shyly. It was nearly two months since he had last seen her, and life with Daddy had been so different that she almost seemed like a stranger. Having gazed at his mother for a few seconds, he climbed on to Freddie's knee and put his arms around his neck as if to reassure Julia that he was happy and well cared for.

Apparently satisfied with what she saw, Julia stood up and moved towards the door.

'It looks as if he's decided to stay,' she said, but as Freddie opened the door for her John leaped after his mother.

'Don't go, Mummy, please,' he sobbed, burying his head in her skirt and making as if to stop her from leaving.

'Look, Julia, for John's sake let's have another go,' pleaded Freddie, still hopeful that they might become a family again.

'It's no use, I don't want to,' was Julia's reply.

'Then John will have to decide for himself,' said Freddie, and turning to John he addressed him slowly and clearly. 'Mummy's going away and she won't be coming back again. Do you want to go with her or stay with me and go to New Zealand?'

Unfalteringly John took his father's hand. 'I'm staying with Daddy,' he said.

Julia didn't speak, but silently opened the front door and began to walk away down the street. Yet before she had gone fifty yards John, not understanding what was happening, wrenched his hand from Freddie's and ran after her, calling, 'Come on, Daddy.'

It was manifestly clear that John had made his decision and that Freddie had no choice but to abide by it. Turning

73

sadly to Mrs Hall, he asked her to pack John's things quickly; her son Billy delivered them to Bobby Dykins, who was waiting uneasily at the end of the avenue. Julia had already disappeared round the corner, with John still clinging tightly to her arm.

Freddie spent the rest of the afternoon walking through the sand dunes where he and John had loved to play, trying to come to terms with the situation. For the first time in his life, except perhaps when he was sent to the orphanage, his irrepressible spirit was extinguished by a gaping emptiness inside. Despite the short periods he had spent with his wife and child, they had represented an important anchor in his life and he had loved them dearly in his own way. Now he felt beset by an unfamiliar sense of loneliness which he found very hard to handle.

Later that evening Mrs Hall entreated him to stop moping and join the rest of the family on an outing to the Cherry Tree, a large pub on the outskirts of Blackpool which they had often visited during Freddie's stay. The Cherry Tree boasted a stage area with a microphone where local talent was invited to perform, and the showbiz atmosphere was enhanced by the frequent appearance of artistes starring in the shows on the Pier or at the Tower. Freddie himself had soon proved popular amongst the regulars as a singer, and had even been approached by a stage manager friend of Billy's who offered him a job as his assistant as a 'stepping stone to the real thing', as he put it.

'I'm afraid I won't be very good company tonight,' he apologized to his companions as they entered the convivial hubbub of the bar, and despite the efforts of his friends to cheer him up his heart remained heavy.

But once the entertainments began, the music and the songs did begin to loosen the knot inside him a little, and when the call for Freddie went out, although he initially refused, Billy Hall was insistent that he should do his usual turn. 'Get up there,' he urged him. 'It'll do you good.'

Instinctively he asked for Al Jolson's number, 'Little Pal', which he would often perform at the ships' concerts complete with black greasepaint, and without thought he found himself substituting 'John' for 'pal'. Neither was he ashamed of his tears, joined by Mrs Hall, as he returned to their table amidst sympathetic clapping and shoulder-patting.

For Freddie the music provided a release for the emotions he found hard to express. And in the weeks and months that followed, he found his thoughts constantly returning to the words of the song. Somehow the lyrics so aptly summed up his feelings – his hopes that John might be 'the man his Daddy might have been' and that they might one day 'meet again, heaven knows where or when'.

4
DADDY, COME HOME

There seemed to be little point in hanging around Blackpool any longer, so the next day Freddie headed back down to Southampton, accompanied by Billy Hall's brother Johnny who was hoping to find work as a ship's steward. They say that time is a great healer, and a period of continuous sailing aboard the *Almanzora* from 29 June 1946 until 13 December 1947, with no chance of signing off, gave Freddie the opportunity to come to terms with the break-up of his home.

Once back in familiar surroundings, however, he felt different. Christmas 1947 was bitterly cold, but it was not really the weather that cast his spirits so low. It was the first time he had been back in Liverpool for eighteen months and it was also the first time he had felt really alone at Christmas, despite a mad round of visits to his friends and relatives. Polly was always overjoyed to see him and for his part she was the only person to whom he could pour out his heart as he helped her with the household chores or shared a pot of tea in the back kitchen just like the old days.

Sydney tried his best to sympathize about the failure of the marriage and even managed to restrain himself from saying 'I told you so' – despite his disappointment that his hopes of adopting John had failed to materialize. They celebrated New Year's Eve together and he was mildly impressed when Freddie went up on stage and sang a few songs – the first time he had seen his brother perform since the Will Murray spectacular at the Empire Theatre. Unfortunately Sydney had no news to report about Julia, of whom nothing had been seen or heard, but at Freddie's insistence he did promise to write to him immediately should he receive information about any change in her situation.

'But why don't you find out where she's living and confront her face to face?' Sydney wanted to know.

'Surely you don't expect me to go knocking on her door when she's living with another man?' exclaimed Freddie indignantly.

'Not even for John's sake?' pressed Sydney, still hopeful that there might be a chance for him and his wife to adopt John.

'She'll come back to me sooner or later,' replied Freddie, dodging the question. As Julia had never asked him for a divorce, he still believed that she might one day tire of Bobby Dykins and that things would eventually be restored to the way they used to be.

The *Andes* was the flagship of the Royal Mail Lines, and on 11 January 1948 was scheduled to make her maiden voyage which had been delayed as a result of the war. The luxurious new cruiser had attracted the cream of the catering staff from all the other top passenger liners, including the *Queen Mary*, so when the opportunity of an assistant steward's job arose Freddie gratefully accepted.

There was no head waiter as such, the dining room being supervised by the maître d'hôtel, Gino, a genius of a man who had a way of manipulating the passengers while leading them to believe that he was pandering to their every whim. The passenger list was also very promising from a waiter's point of view, featuring several members of the racing fraternity who could always be relied upon for good tips – of the betting as well as the cash-in-hand kind. All in all the voyage promised to be great fun, and Freddie felt it would be just the tonic he needed to restore his *joie de vivre*.

But before the ship sailed he called in on the Halls in

Blackpool, who still hoped that he would accompany them to New Zealand where he could forget the past and make a new life for himself.

'I can't miss the chance to sail on a corker of a ship like the *Andes*,' he told them. 'But I'll do a couple of runs and if I still haven't heard anything from Julia I'll join your boys on the Aussie service and meet you over there.'

Although he didn't wish to let down the Halls, he was now somewhat reluctant to emigrate. Once he had left England for good there would be no hope whatsoever of getting back together with Julia and young John.

The destination of the *Andes* was Argentina, and the arrival of the ship in the River Plate was marked by a series of welcomes by large numbers of high-ranking officials and thousands of excited people. In Buenos Aires Eva Peron herself came on board amidst tremendous rejoicing.

However, the jubilation in no way lessened the enthusiasm of the *vigilantes*, the local police, for jailing merchant sailors without charge or hearing. The First and Last was an appropriately named café-bar which formed the hub of all that went on for seamen in Buenos Aires, and it was from here that the *vigilantes* would regularly pick at random twenty to thirty sailors whose identity passes would be taken from them and who would be swiftly thrown in jail. At about ten o'clock the next morning, without any appearance before magistrates, the inmates would be relieved of varying sums of pesetas in return for their release, with the distinct possibility of undergoing the very same procedure the following night. The *vigilantes* were undiscriminating in their choice of detainees, and the only reason why the passengers themselves were never subjected to this indignity was that they had the use of cars to and from the ship.

It was during Freddie's second trip on the *Andes* in the summer of 1948, that he underwent the most terrifying experience of his life as a result of this ritual incarceration. And for the first but certainly not the last time his relationship to John Lennon was to cause him a brush with death.

On this particular night the large cell was almost full when Freddie and six others were bundled in, and they resigned themselves to a cold, sleepless night, thankful that it would only be a few hours before they would be released. But the following morning, when the others were allowed to go and their identity passes were returned to them, Freddie was left in the cell. He remained there all day, without food, until the next night's clients began to arrive. By four o'clock the following day he had still received no food and no visitors except for the arrival of a very early prisoner – either a wino or a mental case – who staggered into the cell, leering and cackling like an idiot, before falling asleep in the corner.

Suddenly, about an hour later, the huddled form in the corner leaped to its feet, emitting the most devilish screech imaginable, and threw itself at Freddie, gibbering and frothing at the mouth. Fortunately he was saved by the entrance of a guard who was bringing in some new clients. He led away the nutcase, who was still screaming and trembling in the throes of some kind of fit.

The new arrivals were from the *Andes*, two stewards and three firemen. They were horrified to learn that Freddie had been held for two days and nights without anything to eat or drink.

'Don't worry, mate,' they reassured him. 'We'll get you out of here by twelve o'clock tomorrow even if we have to bring the whole bloody crew along to free you.'

In fact it was about three o'clock in the afternoon before a guard unlocked the cell and Freddie was taken to the reception office. Tears of relief blurred his vision as he beheld his boss, Mr Cartwright, a big, strong, strapping man, looking as if he were about to tear the place down with his bare hands. And his old mate Jacko also came forward to greet him, endeavouring to force a smile on his worried face as he offered cigarettes, fruit, sandwiches and chocolate

79

which Freddie hungrily devoured.

'My God, am I glad to see you,' he gasped between mouthfuls. 'They've had me here for two days and I don't know what the hell's going on.'

Mr Cartwright had in fact unravelled the mystery with the assistance of a Spanish-speaking steward who acted as interpreter, but the news was far from good.

'You're never going to believe this, son,' explained Mr Cartwright, shaking his head. 'But it seems the bastards want you for murder. They've got the idea from your ship's pass that you're a wanted man.' He pointed to the pass, lying open on the desk, which listed the name of his next of kin, John, and directly beneath, Freddie's own signature, A. Lennon. The name of the murderer the police were looking for was John Alennon, to whom Freddie apparently bore a striking resemblance.

At least another hour passed in wrangling and getting nowhere with the *vigilantes* before his shipmates left him with a hearty handshake and the promise that they would enlist the help of the British consul, a word which brought no relief to Freddie.

He was nevertheless hopeful of release when, at eleven o'clock the next morning, a guard appeared and led him to the reception room. But his optimism was dashed when he was immediately handcuffed and pushed into a Black Maria which transported him to a heavily guarded building about an hour's drive away. Here he was marched up a flight of stone stairs, at every turning of which stood a guard with rifle poised, and thrown into a cell containing a mob of hideous-looking men who were howling for their dinner, which was just about to be served.

'John Alennon,' announced the grim-faced guard by way of introduction.

'No,' shouted Freddie, 'I'm English,' which set the guard into shrieks of derisive laughter.

As the prisoners clamoured for their food, a kind of stew

dished out in scoops into their plates, a short, stocky, villainous-looking man with close-cropped fair hair approached Freddie and handed him a plate.

'Don't move,' he said to him in English, spitting in his face. 'Spit back if you like when I've finished. I'm German and they'll gut me if I appear friendly. What have you done?'

'Nothing,' replied Freddie.

The German simply grunted. 'Then you'll be shot tomorrow for nothing. We're all being transferred to the island for execution.' Then he said, 'I'm going to spit again now,' and Freddie spat in return as he walked away. And then, more or less by instinct, he strode towards the gate with his head held high and demanded his food, a gesture which caused the mob to fall away with a kind of respect, and probably saved him from further molestation.

After a sleepless night spent pacing up and down or dozing in the corner of the stinking cell, Freddie was startled by a voice shouting 'John Alennon', to which he subconsciously responded by moving towards the gates. He was once more escorted by two guards to the interviewing room, where he was stripped naked and again interrogated in Spanish by two officials.

'John Alennon, John Alennon,' repeated one of the officials, pounding the desk in front of him and pointing to Freddie's identity card.

'English, English, you daft bastard,' roared Freddie with as much energy as he could muster, which seemed to produce the desired effect as the other official now began to question him in English.

'Where were you born?'

'Liverpool, England.'

'What year?'

'1912.'

'What's your mother's name?'

'Mary.'

'What's your name?'

'Alfred Lennon.'

At this the Argentines no longer seemed so sure of themselves, so Freddie took advantage of their hesitation by explaining that the name John was his son's name and that A. Lennon was his signature, in which the 'A' stood for Alfred. Slowly the truth began to dawn upon them, and after a few more hours of incarceration he was finally allowed to leave the cell for the last time. His release aroused a number of disgruntled outcries from the mob, but despite their hostility he felt a surge of pity towards them when he remembered the words of the German prisoner. They were all to be shot that very day, and but for the grace of God he too would have been joining them.

There must have been a dozen people waiting for him when he arrived at reception, but it was the sight of Mr Cartwright and his old pal Jacko that broke the fearful tension he had endured for the last three days and he wept like a child.

'It's all right, la, it's all over now,' Jacko consoled him, embracing him like a long-lost brother, 'You've had us going through hell worrying about you.'

'I know what I'd like to do to this shower of Spanish bastards!' was Mr Cartwright's contemptuous comment as his big hands brushed away his own tears.

The consul's car was waiting to escort them back to the *Andes* and it was during the journey that Mr Cartwright, with a comforting arm around Freddie's shoulders, explained to him what had been happening while he was in jail.

'You're a lucky lad, Lennie,' he said. 'The whole bloody crew were out scouring BA looking for you, and it was thanks to them that the captain agreed to delay the ship's sailing until you returned. There can't be many sailors who have held up the *Andes*.'

'I don't know why fate gets me into these goddam messes.

I suppose I'm bloody lucky to have mates like you,' said Freddie with heartfelt thanks.

Fate had also been hard at work in John Lennon's life. Shortly after Julia had collected him from Blackpool, unbeknown to Freddie she returned him once more to the care of her sister Mimi in Woolton. Things had failed to work out at the flat in Gateacre, where John had spent a few weeks with his mother and his 'new Daddy', Bobby Dykins.

The relationship between John and Bobby was obviously going to be rather strained. John, the image of his father, was a constant reminder to Bobby of Julia's former lover, and the child's sullen and rebellious attitude towards his 'stepfather' did little to improve the situation. The usual problems of a step-relationship were further aggravated by the cramped living conditions of the tiny apartment, and when Julia discovered in July 1946 that she was expecting Bobby's child she knew that things could not continue as they were. So when Mimi offered to bring John up, her offer was gratefully accepted. At thirty-two, Julia was anxious to settle down at last in a secure relationship, and it was essential to her that she should make a success of things with her new man. Given the choice between John and Bobby there was no alternative but to choose Bobby, and she was certain that John would be well cared for by her elder sister.

So John settled in at 251 Menlove Avenue where he was to spend the remainder of his childhood with the forty-three-year-old Mimi Smith, the woman who had adored him since his birth and who had now achieved her ambition to rear him as her own. From the material standpoint he had gained considerably: Mimi's home was large and spacious compared to Gateacre or even Newcastle Road. But psychologically he was devastated.

The confusion and disillusionment of the last few months had proved totally bewildering to John. In choosing to be with his mother at the expense of parting from his father he had in fact ended up by losing both his parents, and he must have felt betrayed by circumstances.

His way of coping was to develop and project the strongly macho personality which effectively concealed the pain he was feeling inside and which was to become his trademark. Suddenly he became angry and aggressive in his dealings with other children; at the local school in Woolton, Dovedale Primary, he became involved in almost perpetual fights as he vented his frustrations on his schoolmates.

He also underwent physical changes, and it was shortly after his parting from his parents that his short-sightedness, inherited from his mother, began to show itself. In fact he became severely myopic and needed to wear strong-lensed glasses permanently from that time onwards.

The taunts attracted by his round-framed National Health spectacles only served further to inflame his anger and impel him to instate himself as leader of the pack. This he achieved with comparative ease on account of his quick wits, sharp tongue and total lack of reverence for everything 'respectable', and he soon acquired a circle of admiring followers.

Little was said to John by Mimi regarding the circumstances of his parents' parting, or why he had been assigned to her care. He was simply led to believe that his parents had fallen out of love and that his father had left home while he was still very young. But it was by virtue of what remained unsaid that problems arose for John.

Julia had coped well with the unsettling circumstances of the past year. Once John was installed at Mimi's, she moved out of the flat in Gateacre and returned to Pop Stanley's home at 9 Newcastle Road for a couple of years, where she gave birth to Julia, her first child by Bobby Dykins, on 5 March 1947.

Shortly before the birth of their second child, Jacqueline, a delicate child born two months prematurely, they moved to a council house in Blomfield Road, Allerton, where Julia dedicated herself to housewifely duties. She had finally achieved the domestic security which she had longed for all her life and which Freddie had been unable to give her. By coincidence Bobby Dykins shared the same profession as Freddie – he was a waiter – which inevitably meant that he had to work unsocial hours; but at least he came home to her every night, albeit at a late hour.

Despite her new-found happiness, Julia did not forget her first-born and would pay spasmodic visits to Menlove Avenue to see the young John, to whom she soon became not so much a mother as a glamorous and exciting older sister whose sparkling and extroverted personality appealed immensely to him. Mimi was anxious that John should grow up with a totally untarnished picture of his mother, and she was careful to keep from him those facts about Julia's past which she herself considered to be 'shameful'. But at least John did see Julia fairly regularly and was able to draw his own conclusions about her character.

The situation was completely different with regard to his father. Following that fateful day in June 1946, John was not to see Freddie again throughout his childhood and he received no information about him from Mimi. Although his memories of the past had quickly clouded over, he had vague recollections of having spent time with his father in Blackpool. But no matter how often he pressed his aunt to talk to him about his father she simply pursed her lips and left his questions unanswered. By Mimi's standards Freddie was a failure, and she felt the less said about him the better. The fact that John was beginning to resemble his father in his freedom-loving anti-author-tarianism had presumably escaped her notice. Virtually the whole neighbourhood knew of John's wild behaviour but it appeared that Mimi never found out about it, or if she did she preferred to turn a blind eye. At any rate, in Mimi's house Freddie's name was never mentioned, and to John his father was to remain a puzzling and disturbing enigma.

On his return to Southampton Freddie was informed that Billy Hall and his brother Johnny were staying at the Royal Court Hotel awaiting news of him. Mr and Mrs Hall had already left for Auckland in New Zealand, and it was understood that their two sons and Freddie would join them later, once they had obtained jobs on an 'Aussie run'.

Freddie was still considering the idea of settling in New Zealand, and when a long-distance phone call to Sydney confirmed that there was still no change in Julia's situation he made up his mind to leave England for good. The three of them sailed on the *Dominion Monarch* and Billy jumped ship in Wellington, where he paid the penalty of six weeks' breaking sandstone. His brother Johnny and Freddie were to do one more trip before leaving the ship, as Billy was trying to arrange for them to be accepted in New Zealand without having to do a rock-breaking session.

It was during the next trip in October 1949, on a beautiful spring-like Sunday, that Freddie was sitting on the open deck enjoying the ever-present winds of Wellington when Jock, the second steward, strolled up to him.

'Throw a jacket on, Freddie, and we'll go to the Gresham for a beer,' he suggested.

As they sat talking over drinks Jock disclosed that he would be leaving the ship in London and returning as a passenger to manage a hotel in Australia. He knew of his shipmate's intention to leave the ship next day and join the Halls in Auckland, and the question he put to him hit Freddie like a bombshell.

'You've a son in Liverpool, haven't you, Freddie?' he said. 'Won't you miss him? You're unlikely to see him again once you're fixed up in Auckland.'

The finality of the situation suddenly became clear, and Freddie sensed in his gut that he couldn't leave England without trying to persuade Julia to allow John to accompany him to New Zealand. In the belief that John was still living with his mother he decided there was no alternative but to swallow his pride and confront Julia, regardless of the presence of Dykins. And it was probably to prevent his mind from dwelling on his anxieties that he worked like mad throughout the return voyage to London.

They arrived at King George V Docks in Tilbury at the end of December 1949 with the prospect of returning home for the New Year. Freddie had arranged to travel to Liverpool to stay with his mother whilst making enquiries about John, and as he left the ship on that fateful morning he knew instinctively that something of great significance was about to happen.

He was immensely excited at the prospect of being reunited with his son, yet he just couldn't stomach the idea of facing Julia under the roof she shared with her lover. Maybe it was the need to gain courage which caused him to drink heavily with his five Scouse mates on a long pub crawl up to London. They had just finished a bottle of rum before they came ashore, and by the time they arrived at Fenchurch Street Station they had drunk two more bottles of rum and a dozen or so beers between them. It was Freddie's first visit to London, and like the others he was determined to see the bright lights before he caught the midnight train to Liverpool. They must have visited every pub in Soho, and although they were all seasoned drinkers they had never before been on a binge quite like this one – it was rums all the way.

By the time they reached Oxford Street they were in very high spirits, singing and shouting as they careered merrily across the deserted thoroughfare. Then, standing in front of him inside a huge glass showcase, Freddie espied a most gorgeous red-headed girl dressed in a beautiful evening gown. She reminded him instantly of Julia, and he experienced an overwhelming urge to dance with the lovely creature.

'Come out and dance,' he called out as his mates hammered on the glass.

'She's locked in,' shouted one mate.

'Kick the door in,' said another.

The silence of the deserted street was broken by the loud shattering of glass as Freddie clambered into the shop window to help the boys set free the captive mannequin. He hadn't noticed that four of the boys had gone until he heard the noise of a police car screeching to a halt and a kindly policeman extracted him from the arms of his dancing partner.

He was taken to Great Marlborough Street Police Station where he entertained the staff with a selection of songs from his repertoire whilst an incriminating gash in his leg was stitched. The following morning his memory of the previous night's antics was jolted by the pain of his thumping head and the throbbing cut to his leg, and as the awful truth began to dawn on him he started to worry about the possible repercussions of his revelries.

His anxieties were lessened by the light-hearted attitude of a large, jovial detective who had been appointed to handle the case and who appeared to think the whole affair was one big joke.

'We all enjoyed the one-man cabaret act last night, Scouse,' was the policeman's cheery greeting.

'It must have been one hell of a binge,' responded Freddie, clutching his pounding head. 'And from the look of things I'm going to have to pay for it.'

'Your only problem, Scouse, is that the shop is claiming damages and you and your mate will probably have to pay a big fine on top.'

'I can muster about £100 myself,' explained Freddie. 'And I'm certain my shipmates could raise some more money if it's needed.'

This seemed to satisfy the detective, especially when Freddie explained that he could also leave a weekly allotment from his pay, and he advised him that he should get off fairly lightly.

The conversation at the court that afternoon focussed on the sentences that were likely to be imposed. However, as Freddie and his mate were first-timers and only up on a drunk charge they were passed over as of no interest by the majority of the regulars. 'A bloody fine,' was the general consensus. But just before the session began their confidence was dashed by a visit from the detective.

'Don't worry too much, boys,' he confided. 'But you've got the worst possible magistrate, he's a VC.' The exclamations of disgust from the regulars seemed to confirm the detective's comment.

'You know what the VC stands for – Very Cruel,' said one. 'He's a moody bastard, and if he's having one of his bad days we'll all be in for long sentences.'

'Military man, you know,' explained another. 'Thinks everyone without rank is a potential criminal.'

As soon as he entered the court room, accompanied by one of his shipmates, Freddie realized that the magistrate's mood was far from lenient. His face appeared stern, brooding and forbidding – not the sort of face, thought Freddie, for a man with the power to dispense justice and to influence the future prospects of the lives of his fellow men.

The damage and the fine were estimated at £250 and the magistrate's assessment was short and blunt.

'I don't think either of you could pay the damage and a fine, so I must sentence you both to six months in jail. Next case, please.'

With the words of the magistrate still echoing in his head, Freddie was led away in a state of numb shock. It was not until three days after he had started his sentence at Wormwood Scrubs that the impact of his position really hit him.

The tragic irony of the situation was that he had returned to England in order to ask for custody of John, yet he had hardly set foot on English soil before he had made a bloody mess of things yet again. A six-month jail sentence seemed hardly likely to improve his credentials as a potential guardian, and neither was it likely to impress Julia. His immediate reaction was to seek Mimi's advice, and when he was given one sheet of paper to write to whomsoever he wished, it was to Mimi that he addressed his letter. He chose his words carefully, confiding his predicament but explaining that he still intended to ask Julia to allow him to take John to New Zealand. With her sound common sense Mimi had always been able to offer practical advice in the past, and despite his merciless teasing of her he had always had a certain respect for her and she for him.

But it was clear from her reply that a change had occurred in her attitude towards him. She had not forgiven Freddie for 'kidnapping' John four years earlier, since when she had lived in continuous fear that he might reappear to claim custody of his son. Mimi had never been granted legal guardianship of John and she was only too well aware that, as his natural father, Freddie could turn up at any time to snatch the boy away to the other side of the world and there would be little that she could do about it. For her own security as John's guardian it was essential that Freddie should be kept well away from his son, and in view of his recent jail sentence she felt perfectly justified in writing to him in stern tones, informing him that John was now living with her and advising him to keep out of his son's life.

'You must resign yourself to the fact that you have now completely severed any hopes you may have had of obtaining custody of the boy,' she wrote. 'You have made an absolute shambles of your life and have brought shame and scandal upon your family. If you have a shred of decency left in you I advise you to go to New Zealand alone and put your past life behind you.' The final sentence was both a command and a threat: 'Surely you don't want your son to know you've been in jail.'

Freddie's immediate reaction was to feel angry with

90

himself for having written to Mimi in the first place. He should have known that she would revert to her strait-laced values and would feel nothing but contempt for him now that he was a 'jail bird'.

But despite his disgust with Mimi's attitude, her cruel words sparked off a sense of self-shame. In the days and weeks that followed, his thoughts kept returning to the letter and the humiliating realization that this time he had really blown it. With a prison record behind him, he felt totally powerless to contest Mimi's refusal to allow him custody of John; his sister-in-law now had him precisely where she wanted him.

But worst of all was the sense that he had completely let John down. For the first time in his life Freddie bowed to propriety and allowed respectability to dictate his actions. Maybe it was better that John should grow up in the suburban security of Menlove Avenue than that he should be snatched away from Mimi to face an uncertain future with a father who could only cause him embarrassment and for whom he might only feel shame. If only he had known of the anti-establishment attitudes that John was even then developing, his decision might well have been different.

As always, the quickest and easiest remedy was to return to sea, and it was with this in mind that Freddie headed straight for the Merchant Navy Pool in London on the day of his release four months later. The *Dominion Monarch* had made it clear that they hadn't any intention of taking him back. 'But don't worry, Lennon,' said the Pool manager. 'With your experience you shouldn't have any trouble in getting a ship. In fact we have a job available right now – provided the union will agree.'

His reception at the union building was less welcoming, however. Having examined his union book, the official at the window gave him a sideways look and yelled out to an unseen figure: 'Hey Pete, that Lennon guy's here.' A hugely fat individual slouched into view, noisily chewing a mammoth-sized sandwich. 'Whath yer wonth?' he gobbled.

Freddie waited patiently for him to finish, but before he could answer he had unceremoniously stuffed another huge lump into his mouth. Not being in a position to show his revulsion, Freddie cautiously enquired whether he should return after lunch. He was sorry he spoke, for he was showered with fragments of wet bread as the fellow replied, 'Done bother, we done carry trath like you.'

Freddie felt like exploding, but an iron grille separated him from his tormentor who, having at last emptied his mouth and feeling safe behind the barrier, finally put in the knife.

'You might as well go,' he said. 'We don't intend to help your kind, and if there's any trouble I'll call the police.'

Freddie was suddenly face to face with the hopeless position an ex-prisoner finds himself in when attempting to resume normal life, and he wondered what people like the magistrate who had sentenced him would do if they could foresee the results of their inexplicable sentences on first offenders.

Over a drink he contemplated his future. He couldn't very well remain down in London any longer, so he decided to hitch-hike to Liverpool. It was about ten o'clock on a beautiful May morning when he arrived at his mother's house. The door was opened by his brother Charlie, whose opening words almost rooted him to the spot.

'Where have you been?' he began. 'We've been trying to contact you. Mother died a couple of months ago.'

It seemed to Freddie that for some curious reason every last shred of security was being snatched from him, as all those anchors which had formed the foundations of his life and which had meant so much to him were suddenly stripped away.

The loss of his mother was really the final blow, for although he had not seen her for two years or more he had always had the knowledge that he could return home any time for a hug, a plate of Scouse and some down-to-earth wisdom. And despite long periods of parting he had felt that she always accompanied him throughout his journeying far and wide – like the night in the Casbah when she had guided his steps in the right direction, or the many other occasions when he had received intuitive warnings about danger.

He thought back to the happy days he had spent with Polly whenever he was home on shore leave, when he would give her a hand with the housework or they would sit down over a cup of tea, laughing till their sides ached over her tales of life with the 'Old Man'. But despite the fun and jokes she had always been a stern disciplinarian, and during his childhood it was from his mother that Freddie had acquired his obsession with principles. Although a cane hung ominously on the wall of the back kitchen it was more of a deterrent than for actual use, except for one occasion when the seven-year-old Freddie had helped himself to a penny from the housekeeping money and had received a few short sharp strokes. It was the one and only occasion that he had ever let his mother down, and his sense of shame had been enormous.

Now at least he was saved the humiliation of having to confess to her about his jail sentence. Now at any rate she would never know where he had been. And that was the one ray of light that helped a little to lessen his grief.

He remained in Liverpool at his mother's house for a period and visited the Seamen's Union to ask for help in finding a ship. But another door was about to close in his face.

'You've spoilt your chances by going to the union in London,' explained the regretful official. 'If you'd been born in the south they would have helped you at the London office, but seeing you're from Liverpool you should have come up here first. If you'd come straight here everything would have been OK, but there's nothing we can do now to change their ruling.'

It seemed to Freddie, looking back, that fate had dealt him a threefold blow. Within the space of a couple of years he had not only lost his wife, his child and his beloved mother, but also his very livelihood and the greatest passion of his life, the sea.

Suddenly there seemed to be nothing left worth living for, and for a short time he became a 'gentleman of the road', travelling up and down the country carrying his worldly possessions with him and occasionally doing a day's work to replenish his stock of necessities. The contacts he made at that time were some of the most interesting of his life and he met many intellectuals or others who, like himself, were disgusted with the workings of society and had sought to opt out.

One Yorkshireman he met had been a journalist of note in Huddersfield and was writing his experiences of the 'Toby' (the road) as he went along. Another had been a surgeon who never talked of his past but still carried his doctor's bag with him and would tend anyone in distress. He met lawyers and businessmen who were fully content to be away from it all, and he felt certain that the freedom of mind and body they had attained by a life on the road more than compensated for any material gains they may have forsaken.

But with the advent of the cold weather he became keen to find bed and board for the winter, and so he accepted a job as a kitchen porter washing dishes in a hotel in the Midlands. Despite the humble nature of the work he was surprised how content he was in the job. He had his own room, an average of £10 a week in his pocket, and his work carried few responsibilities. He was in fact his own boss, provided he kept the kitchens supplied with clean pots and pans.

And so began a new phase in his life. He had inherited Polly's fatalistic outlook on life, and accepted the misfortunes he had experienced without bitterness. 'It wasn't that

I became disenchanted with life itself,' he told me later. 'It was just that I was sickened by the hypocritical attitudes of certain individuals, and from that time onwards I decided to drop out.'

From then on he took the most menial jobs available which afforded him the means to live without being swept up into the vortex of the human rat race. He was a bohemian without really realizing it – a hippie ahead of his time. His only lasting regret was the loss of his wife and child, and he often dreamed a beautiful dream that one day he might yet fall in love again, that he might yet have another little boy to replace the son named John whom he believed he would never see again.

If Freddie Lennon had 'dropped out' of society during this period, then John Lennon was fast following in his footsteps. In 1952 he had started at Quarry Bank High School, where his career as a rabble-rouser progressed steadily. He soon gained a reputation for being 'trouble' amongst the masters, by whom he was largely disliked for his sarcasm and wise-cracks, but surprisingly he managed to survive Quarry Bank with no more than one suspension. Just like Freddie, he seemed to attract trouble wherever he went, but whereas John was usually the one who didn't get caught, Freddie on the other hand always seemed to end up taking the rap. Unlike John, Freddie was naively honest and it was his extraordinary obsession with 'principle' which usually landed him in it.

John's kindly Uncle George Smith died suddenly in 1953, and to replace his lost confidant John began visiting Julia more frequently. Over at Allerton he was able to indulge freely in the kind of relaxed lifestyle that was so obviously absent in Menlove Avenue. He spent most of his time there playing records on his mother's gramophone, listening to rock and roll which had just hit the UK.

He obtained a guitar in 1956 and, having learnt to strum

out some rock and roll chords with Julia's assistance, formed a group with some school friends which he called the Quarry Men. At last he had found a creative outlet for his macho personality, and the next two years of his life were spent developing his skills under the guidance of Paul McCartney who, although two years younger than John, was already an accomplished musician.

Things seemed to be going well when Julia was knocked down and killed by a car whilst crossing Menlove Avenue on a visit to Mimi on 15 July 1958. She died of her injuries before the ambulance reached the hospital. The unexpectedness of her death seemed in keeping with her unpredictable nature, yet proved an almost incomprehensible shock to those who loved her.

Bobby Dykins was totally distraught and for a while found it hard to cope with life. Julia had inspired a passionate devotion in all who fell under her spell, and for Bobby the past twelve years had represented the most blissfully happy period of his life. The only shadow had been cast by the fact that they had never been able to marry, since they had been unsuccessful in obtaining Freddie's consent to a divorce, despite several attempts to do so. As a result their little girls had been born out of wedlock, although few people were aware of the fact, as Julia and the children always used the name Dykins.

But now, with Julia's death, it seemed that Bobby had lost the whole reason for his existence, and curiously the girls proved of little comfort to him. He felt unable to handle the day-to-day care of young Julia and Jacqueline, and when it was suggested that they should go to live with their Aunt Harriet, close to Mimi's home in Woolton, he gratefully accepted the offer. He slowly recovered from his grief and eventually remarried, but by a strange quirk of fate he too suffered a violent death: in 1966 he was killed in a car crash whilst returning to Liverpool from Wales.

Fate was also establishing an extraordinary link between

the lives of Julia's three children. Just as John had been effectively orphaned in 1946 by the disappearance from his life of first his father and then his mother, so too young Julia and Jacqueline were to lose both their parents within the space of eight years, whilst they were still of a tender age.

For John himself, Julia's death signalled the onset of a further phase of embittered aggression. He was hopeful that his father might turn up for the funeral, and felt deeply disappointed when he didn't. At the age of seventeen the realization hit him that he would never see either of his parents again, and he felt immensely isolated. Unlike his half-sisters he found it impossible to give expression to his grief, and he simply pushed down his feelings into the depths of his subconscious as he had done many times during his childhood when personal tragedies had befallen him. Over the years John had become adept at blocking his tears.

To compensate for the denial of his sorrow, his macho personality became even more exaggerated. Not only did his wit take a particularly cruel turn, the butt of which was often the afflicted and disabled, but he also began to drink heavily, giving his tongue an even sharper and cruder edge. It seemed that John felt nothing but anger and contempt for everyone in his environment, which he openly expressed without any regard for those to whom he might cause suffering. Yet, strangely, Mimi remained the one person to whom he deferred.

Despite the rapidly widening gap between her prudish respectability and John's growing taste for vulgarity, it was only she who escaped the venom of his vicious sarcasm. It is curious that such a strait-laced woman should be drawn to a lad whose artistic endeavours were eventually to include a photograph of his own penis in erection; even more curious that they should experience such devotion to one another. It seemed that they were bonded by a force beyond blood ties.

The tragedy of his mother's death was nevertheless to

endow John with a new-found energy and determination. He cast himself into his music with gritty determination, and the tortured laments of rock provided a much-needed release for his pent-up feelings. Like his father before him, he found in music a welcome outlet for the emotions he was unable to express overtly.

His response to the blows life had dealt him was a defiant two-fingered gesture and the resolution to 'show 'em'. Whereas Freddie's reaction had been simply to drop out and to turn his back on society, John's answer was the reverse. His ambition to become rich and famous now crystallized and, as if it were by mind over matter, he began willing himself to make an impact on the world that none other had achieved before him.

It was while he was working at the Barn Restaurant in Solihull with his brother Charlie that Freddie heard about Julia's death. On the Tuesday after the Bank Holiday he received a letter from his elder brother Sydney, enclosing a cutting of an article from the *Liverpool Echo* which reported the accident.

Memories of all their crazy, fun-filled days together began to crowd back into his mind, and although it was some eleven years since he had last seen Julia he experienced a sudden emptiness inside him. He felt the need to be alone with his thoughts, and with the manager's condolences he took the rest of the day off to reminisce.

It was obviously too late for him to pay his respects at her funeral, and so he thought it best for all concerned if he remained incognito as he had done for so many years in the past. He still found it hard to believe that he and Julia could have parted after all they had going for them. But it seemed that things had worked out between her and Bobby Dykins, as she was clearly still living with him at the time of her accident.

It was then that Charlie remarked that there had been

several callers at 27 Copperfield Street asking for Freddie during the past few years. 'They wanted to persuade you to give Julia a divorce,' he explained. 'And one of them was even offering £500, but I told them to get lost.'

Because he had never heard to the contrary, Freddie had never suspected that Julia was interested in a divorce. He felt a pang of regret. He heard that she had given birth to two girls while living with Bobby Dykins, and for their sake as well as Julia's he would willingly have released her from the marriage had he known.

Unsettled by the news of Julia's death, he handed in his notice and hit the road for London in an attempt to put the past behind him once more. But fate was waiting for him yet again and he broke his leg just in time for Christmas, forcing him to spend the festive season in a Sally Army hostel, barely managing on sick pay and with very little to feel cheerful about.

It was while he was staying at the hostel that he received a letter from a firm of Liverpool solicitors informing him that his wife had left a sum of money which he was entitled to inherit as he was the next of kin. 'But there are a number of obstacles to your receiving the money,' the letter continued. 'Several of your wife's relatives have filed a claim and are challenging your right to inherit.'

'And you don't need to be a Philadelphia lawyer to realize just who those relatives might be,' Freddie remarked to Charlie on the phone.

What struck Freddie most forcibly was that Mimi had been able to track him down so easily in the middle of London at this time. Yet she had apparently been unable to contact him when Julia met with her fatal accident, and he had been left to discover the news weeks later in a press report.

He celebrated the New Year by having the plaster removed from his leg, and with his trusty stick as companion he hitch-hiked to Liverpool to enquire of the solicitors exactly what was expected of him.

He felt it would be unprincipled of him to accept his dead wife's money, but neither had he any intention of allowing Mimi to get her hands on it. It seemed to him that the only just course of action was that John should receive the inheritance, and it was with this intention that he arrived at the solicitors' offices in Dale Street on the Saturday morning. They were clearly expecting his visit, but it rather took the wind out of their sails when he informed them of his purpose.

'My only interest in the matter is to see that my son John receives the money,' he explained. 'And under no circumstances will I sign anything which would enable Mimi Smith to inherit it.'

They then showed him a document listing the names of Mimi and her sisters, who had all filed claims to the paltry sum. And although he laughed at the time and remarked 'What a cheek', he later confided to Charlie that he was disgusted. Despite his happy-go-lucky, unrecriminating outlook, from that time onwards he only ever spoke of Mimi with avid dislike.

5
THE PRODIGAL FATHER

In the summer of 1963 the Beatles had reached the top of the charts with 'She Loves You', their third consecutive number one hit, and the name of John Lennon was front page news throughout the country. John had come a long way since the days of the Quarry Men, and his natural talent and charisma were being groomed for world fame under the astute business acumen of Brian Epstein.

That summer found Freddie working as a kitchen porter in the Moor Place Hotel at Esher on the outskirts of London, whilst unbeknown to him his long-lost son was heading for the peaks of stardom. For the last decade or so the laughing had come to a stop for Freddie, and he had lived through the toughest and most depressing period of his life. But now, with a steady job and a secure roof over his head, his spirits began to rise once more. And indeed it was while he was working at the Moor Place that he began to break into song again, for no real reason other than the pleasant atmosphere that prevailed in the kitchen regardless of how hard the work was.

Most of the time he aided the chef single-handed, but on the evenings when there were special dinner parties or wedding receptions to be catered for he was provided with help from some of the local women. There was one old dear in particular who was constantly urging him to 'sing up' as they ploughed through an immense pile of plates, coffee cups and teapots. And on one of these evenings, when Freddie had just arrived at the deafening finale of one of the numbers from his repertoire, she remarked with a wink:

'You sound just like that group of lads from Liverpool, the Beatles.'

At the time the comment made very little impact on Freddie since he had never even heard of the Beatles – or any other group for that matter. He possessed neither television nor radio, and usually spent his day off enjoying a pint and a game of darts in the local pub or an occasional trip to the races. A few days later, however, the same woman brought up the subject again.

'Hey, Freddie, did you know that one of them Beatle boys is named Lennon like yourself? Perhaps he's some relation of yours – he certainly looks the spitting image of you.' Once again, this information had little effect on Freddie. Not for one moment did he associate the name with himself, and as their conversation wasn't overheard the subject was never raised again while he remained at the Moor Place.

But by the winter of 1963 the full force of Beatlemania had finally unleashed itself on Britain and within a couple of months the United States had also fallen under its spell. In December 'I Wanna Hold Your Hand' zoomed to number one immediately on its release with unprecedented advance orders of one million copies, and a total of seven Beatle records featured in the British top twenty.

Never before had such adulation existed amongst the young for any performing artists, and it was towards John that the main thrust of the hysteria was directed. He was fast achieving his long-standing ambition to become wealthy and famous, but the suddenness of his rise to riches and the fervour of the millions of insatiable fans was staggering – even to him.

Never a day passed that a leading article on the Beatles did not appear in the national dailies, and however hard Freddie attempted to bury his head in the sand his son's face confronted him from every news-stand. Slowly the thought began to occur to him that Beatle John might indeed be his own little John, but as no details of John's family

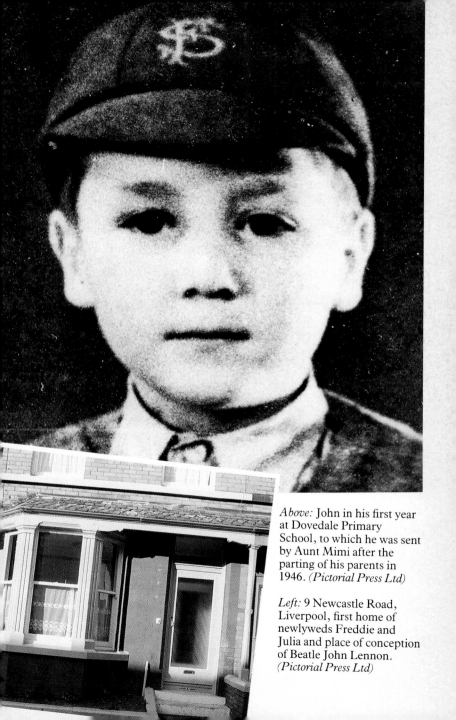

Above: John in his first year at Dovedale Primary School, to which he was sent by Aunt Mimi after the parting of his parents in 1946. *(Pictorial Press Ltd)*

Left: 9 Newcastle Road, Liverpool, first home of newlyweds Freddie and Julia and place of conception of Beatle John Lennon. *(Pictorial Press Ltd)*

Left: Mimi Smith – the devoted aunt who cared for John from the age of six and who Freddie felt had kept his son from him. *(Pictorial Press Ltd)*

Right: Polly Lennon (John's paternal grandmother) pictured at the end of a hard life as a widowed mother in pre-war working class Liverpool during which she was allowed to see her grandson John only once. *(Stone)*

Left: The guardianship of the young John Lennon was hotly contested. Uncle Sydney Lennon, like Mr and Mrs Hall of Blackpool, lost out to Aunt Mimi in his attempt to adopt John. *(Stone)*

Right: Married to the sea? Despite his lengthy absences from home, Freddie (pictured here aged about thirty-three) was still hopeful that he might keep his young family together. *(Stone)*

Above: An ill-matched couple? Freddie and I surprised the world by marrying despite our thirty-five year age gap, by having a child David (pictured with Freddie top) and by remaining together until the end of Freddie's life. *(Stone)*

Left: The Oldest Teenager in the World – Freddie aged fifty-four smiling with happiness at the time of his first reunion with John. *(Stone)*

Above: 'Kenwood', John's
luxurious home in Weybridge,
Surrey, where he hoped his father
would spend his retirement years
in quiet repose. But the
irrepressible Freddie had other
plans! *(Pictorial Press Ltd)*

Right: Uncle Charlie Lennon,
Freddie's loyal and plain-speaking
younger brother, whose timely
letter to John led directly to the
first reconciliation between the
Beatle and his father. *(Stone)*

Above: John in contemplative mood. By the summer of 1967 John was ready to begin talking to his father and it was here, in the sun-room at Kenwood, that their first discussions took place. *(Rex Features Ltd)*

Left: John with Julian, the son he came to believe he had treated almost as badly as Freddie had treated him as a child. *(Rex Features Ltd)*

Kenwood.
Cavendish Rd
Weybridge
Surrey.

Dear Alf Fred Dad Pater whatever

It's the first of your letters
I've read without feeling strange — so
here I am answering it — ok? As you
know I'm pretty tied up at the moment
I've a lot of. Lot to do — if I get time
I'll give Uncle ? Charlie a ring — but
anyway I'll get in touch with you before
a month has passed — after Xmas I'm going
to India a couple of months so I'll
try and make sure we meet before then. I
know it will be a bit awkward when we
first meet and maybe for a few meetings
but there's hope for us yet! I'm glad
you didn't land yourself with a bloody big
family — it's put me off seeing you a little
more — I've enough family to last me
a few life times — write if you feel like
it
John

P.S. Don't spread it 	I don't want Mimi cracking up!
(press I mean).

John's first letter to his father, written in September 1967, just six days after the
death of Brian Epstein and a few weeks after his meeting with the Maharishi
Mahesh Yogi. (Stone)

⊕ wonderful
Weybridge

Dear Freddie + Pauline,

Got your letter — sorry
to hear about the baby — but glad
to hear your both happy. theres
nothing much to say really — Indica
was good — but glad to get back to
work. Would love to come and visit
you both — Julian digs the seaside.
Give me a ring when your plugged
in. — watch your arse in Brighton
— loads of queers! Anyway write if
you feel like
                with love
                    John ⊕

NEW
Phone No} WEYBRIDGE 4 7776.
this papers a drag to write on.

Always a man of few words: the only hint in this letter that John was about to
leave his wife and child for Yoko Ono was the announcement of his new
telephone number – a sure sign of imminent publicity. *(Stone)*

background had as yet appeared in the press reports he had no way of being certain.

Of course there could be no doubt that the physical resemblance was strong. The inherited Irish good looks were undeniable – the same finely chiselled nose with the slightly flared nostrils, the same high cheekbones, the same bushy eyebrows framing almond-shaped eyes; and above all the same expression of arrogance and superiority. There was, though, something much harder about John's face than Freddie's, and the sparkle of fun and laughter was curiously absent.

As Freddie thought back to the fair-haired little boy who had sat on his knee and called him Daddy it hardly seemed conceivable that he could have matured into this charismatic and talented young man. It was true that he had always been a confident youngster, even precocious for his years, but he had never shown any signs of being interested in music when he was a kiddie, unlike Freddie himself who had begun performing at an early age. Yet showbiz and music certainly ran in the Lennon family, and it gave Freddie a curious sort of thrill to think that John Lennon might have inherited his talent from himself.

But there was a bitter-sweet aspect to this revelation. It would have been good to acknowledge his pride in his son and to shake him heartily by the hand. But after so many years' absence he felt he could only prove an embarrassment to John, and there would be really no alternative but to maintain a low profile and to keep out of his life.

With his mind in turmoil at these disquieting thoughts Freddie arrived just before Christmas 1963 at the Grasshopper Inn near Caterham, where he was to take up a new job as a kitchen porter – or KP as it was called in the trade.

Here it was only a matter of days before he was approached by the chef, who had immediately spotted the obvious connection between John Lennon and Freddie. It was over a drink in the bar one evening after work that he confronted Freddie with his suspicions.

'You're John Lennon's father, aren't you?' he asked outright.

'Not to my knowledge,' Freddie replied.

'You're a fool if you keep it to yourself. You're the image of him,' he insisted. 'Your name's Lennon, you come from Liverpool, why the hell don't you admit you're related to him?'

'Look, I did have a son named John but I haven't seen him since his mother left me for another man, and that was seventeen years ago,' explained Freddie. 'I suppose he could be my son, but I've no way of knowing. And what if he is? He won't bloody well be interested in me after all this time, will he?'

But it was obvious that the chef didn't intend to let the matter rest. Word of his identity was soon around the village and the landlady of the local pub, the Sun, which she had won in a *Daily Sketch* competition, took him discreetly aside one evening.

'I have the name of a reporter on the *Sketch* who I know would handle your story with the utmost confidence – should you decide to sell it, of course,' she whispered. Freddie declined, but that was not the end of things.

A few days after Christmas he was looking forward to his first day off after a particularly hectic schedule in the kitchen. He was just leaving to catch the bus to London when the chef drew up in his small car.

'I wrote to the *News of the World* about you,' he called out, waving a letter in his hand. 'But they don't want to know,' he added ruefully. 'They say there's nothing more left to write about the Beatles.'

'Thank heavens for that,' replied Freddie, angry that the chef had contacted the press without his permission. And in a state of exasperation he marched straight to the manager's office, announced that he was fed up with the job and asked for his cards.

It seemed to Freddie that he would be unable to get any peace until he had once and for all cleared up the question of John Lennon's identity. So his first step was to visit his brother Charlie, who was still working at the Barn in Solihull, to ask him what he knew of the matter. Charlie's first greeting, however, was sufficient to erase any doubts. 'You know that John Lennon the Beatle is your son, don't you?' he asked bluntly. 'The papers are running stories that you abandoned him as a baby. What the hell are you going to do about it?'

There could now be no denying that he was indeed John's father, but despite the derogatory press reports he felt disinclined to make himself known. He remained in Birmingham long enough to arrange a new KP job down south, and by the end of January he was safely tucked away from the world in an exclusive but homely hotel in Bognor Regis. The hotel provided a perfect refuge from which he resolved never to emerge again – if he could help it.

Alas for Freddie, the desired peace was not to be. A couple of months after his arrival at his hideaway, just when he was beginning to feel completely relaxed and in harmony with one and all, a letter arrived from his brother Sydney. The tone of the letter was aggressive and accused Freddie of threatening to take his story to the press. 'You can bring your son nothing but shame,' it went on. 'The best thing you can do is to keep out of his life completely and stop bothering him.' The final rebuke was even more inexplicable. 'Why don't you get out and work for a living?' the letter ended. Surely Sydney didn't think that he was a resident at the hotel?

It was hard for Freddie to understand why Sydney had confronted him with an accusation of this kind. He was, of course, aware that Sydney had been angry with him for years for having 'broken his promise' to allow him to adopt John. According to Charlie, Syd had felt betrayed when he heard that John was living with Mimi and held Freddie responsible for the disappointment he and his wife had suffered. But surely this was not the reason for the reprimanding letter?

The irony of the situation was that Freddie had deliberately avoided making known his relationship with John and had refrained from making any contact with the newspapers. The only approach made to the press – albeit without his knowledge – had been that of the chef at the Grasshopper Inn to the *News of the World*. But how could Sydney have come to hear of this?

His first reaction was a compulsive urge to right the injustice and clear his name of these unfounded attacks. There was no alternative but to pack in his job once again and travel to Liverpool in order to demand an explanation from Sydney.

He broke his journey in Solihull to show Charlie the insulting letter and to confide to him his sense of outrage and anger.

'You know what really makes me mad?' he confessed. 'It's the fact that I'm being accused of a crime I haven't committed. You know I've said nothing to the press.'

'Yes, although you bloody well should have done,' remarked Charlie. 'The papers have been full of lies about you walking out on your wife and kid. I know what I'd have done if I'd been in your position.'

Charlie decided to accompany his brother to Liverpool, suggesting that Sydney might be more disposed to talk to himself than to Freddie. But Syd refused point-blank to discuss anything with either of them and Freddie was finally obliged to tackle him in the street outside the mens' outfitting shop where he worked.

In full view and earshot of all passers by, Freddie then proceeded to harangue Sydney for a full five minutes as he scuttled up the London Road with Freddie in hot pursuit. In Freddie's eyes Sydney had treated him contemptuously and fully deserved to be 'told his fortune', as he put it.

106

Sydney, always a stickler for keeping up appearances, was unable to forgive his brother for this public humiliation and never spoke to him again.

Calculating that there would be little point in visiting Mimi, Freddie had written her a letter demanding a full explanation of what she knew of the affair. But a few days later she had sent back the letter – opened – in an envelope.

'I recognized your writing,' read the enclosed note. 'So I am returning your letter without having read it.'

'It seems bloody funny that neither Mimi nor Syd will speak to us,' commented Charlie. 'They've always been two of a kind.'

Freddie and Charlie spent Christmas and the New Year in a guest house in Mount Pleasant, Liverpool but there was little Yuletide peace or good cheer in store for them. The name and the face were an immediate giveaway, and curious eyes and wagging tongues followed Freddie wherever he went. The defamatory stories circulating in the media were becoming increasingly venomous, but Freddie's efforts to clear his name sank under the avalanche of public adoration now descending upon John.

Worse, he was frequently confronted by large crowds of teenagers who had recognized him as John's father and who plagued him with the most embarrassing and unanswerable questions. He felt that he had almost reached breaking point, and with a heavy heart he returned once more to London.

It was early on a cold winter's morning and Freddie was sitting in one of his favourite cafés in London, close to the Scala Theatre, sipping hot tea and contemplating his next move. He had just decided on another cuppa before visiting the catering agency for a live-in job when he was startled by an unusual amount of noise for that time of the morning. So, draining his cup to the dregs, he strolled out into the pale, sunlit street where the cause of the rumpus was now visible.

A horde of screaming, yelling teenagers were milling round the Scala, chanting non-stop: 'We want the Beatles.' Many of them were also trying to climb the building in an effort to force their way in or to look through the windows to catch sight of the 'adorable four'.

As Freddie stood on the pavement opposite surveying the unbelievable scene, a bowler-hatted city gent paused in his hurried stride to the office and addressed him in disgusted tones.

'Do you know what I'd like to do to those Beatles?'

Freddie shook his head.

'I'd hang the noisy bastards up by their long hair.' He obviously wasn't a fan.

He strode on without waiting for a reply – but then what reply could Freddie have made? In the first place he himself sported long hair like any true 'toby trotter'. And had he revealed that one of the 'noisy bastards' was his son, the city gent might well have set about him with his umbrella!

But the caustic remark brought home to Freddie the humour of the situation. He imagined for a moment what would be the result if he were to struggle through the seething mob and announce to the panting policemen: 'I'm John Lennon's father. May I go in?' He could visualize himself being carted off to the nearest nuthouse!

Yet the more he thought about it, the more convinced he became that see John he must, to explain that he hadn't any intention of pestering him and would be thankful just for the opportunity of saying 'Good luck, son', although he was also aware that even that intention would be misconstrued by some. Thoughts of his intended visit to the catering agency had now been dispelled as he stood around fascinated by the antics of the teenagers and hoping, like them, to catch a glimpse of the boys when they came out. But eventually he became bored with the unreality of the situation and returned to the café for another cup of tea.

Half an hour later he had made up his mind. He would

108

attempt to arrange a meeting with John before the libellous stories about him forced him to sue – which he was sure would cause John even more embarrassment than a face-to-face confrontation with his long-lost father.

He traversed Fleet Street for hours on end, mentally rehearsing his approach, when he suddenly remembered the name of the reporter on the *Daily Sketch* given to him by the landlady of the Sun pub in Caterham. Deciding to take the bull by the horns, he marched into the *Sketch* office and asked for the reporter by name.

Needless to say, the journalist was at first far from convinced that Freddie was who he claimed to be. He didn't exactly look down and out, but his obvious lack of assets was hardly what one expected of the parent of a megastar.

'How in the name of Jesus do you expect me to believe that you're John Lennon's father?' was his first dubious appraisal.

'Look, if you don't believe me I can easily go elsewhere,' retorted Freddie abruptly, and the interview was nearly brought to a sudden and premature end.

'Hang on, old man, hang on', blurted out the confused newspaper man, anxious not to foul up a bloody good exclusive. And over a beer and more gentle questioning he eventually extracted positive proof that Freddie was indeed the father of Beatle John.

The chaotic activity which ensued precipitated Freddie into a whirl of surreptitious goings-on that were to land him, three days later, in the presence of his eminence John. Following further intensive interrogation he was ensconced in the Hotel Clarendon where he was left in the charge of two reporters – no doubt in case he made a bolt for freedom.

Then, for three whole days, he was driven each morning in a window-draped car to the vicinity of the Scala Theatre where, closely guarded by the two reporters, he was allowed to visit a nearby pub while Operation John was mounted. And on the third day it came to pass that the two jubilant reporters careered into the pub yelling 'Success, success, we've done it, Freddie' – it seemed that the world-shattering interview had at last been arranged.

But the bizarre farce had not yet ended and Freddie was propelled once again into the draped automobile and driven round London at least a dozen times – no doubt to confuse him as to the exact location of his destination. But as they failed to cover his head with the obligatory coat, he realized they weren't five minutes' walk away from the Scala. He was then whisked out of the car so quickly that he hardly noticed whether it was night or day and was pushed into a tradesmen's lift which went up one floor.

It was on the way to the meeting that one of the reporters gave Freddie a description of the John Lennon his fans knew little about.

'He's a hard case, Freddie,' he was told. 'Don't expect him to be friendly. He's as likely to give you a punch on the nose as to want to shake your hand.'

'Well, in that case he would most assuredly receive two back,' was Freddie's retort, at which the reporter rubbed his hands together gleefully. 'It's a bloody shame we can't take our cameras in,' he remarked.

The first person Freddie saw on leaving the lift was the Beatles' manager, Brian Epstein.

'This way,' he smiled affably as he opened a sliding door through which the three other Beatles emerged, leaving John alone in the room behind them. The serious-faced George cast his eyes away from Freddie's, but Ringo gave him a knowing wink which intimated 'Don't worry.' And finally Paul signalled his acknowledgement of the occasion by a mischievous grin and a friendly squeeze of Freddie's arm as he passed him by.

The door slid silently shut behind them, leaving father and son alone together for the first time in eighteen years. John was lolling languidly on a kind of divan, but Freddie detected immediately that he was far from composed. And Freddie himself found his heart pounding as he stood face-to-face with the child who had now become a grown man and who seemed almost totally unfamiliar to him. For a moment they surveyed each other as strangers, yet with the awareness of their special bond. The silence was broken by John.

'What do you want, then?' he snapped, as taut as a tiger before his final leap.

Freddie took his cue from John's fixed expression and realized he must attempt to relieve the tension.

'I don't want anything,' Freddie replied. 'Certainly not to jump on the band wagon, no matter what you've heard. I just want to make it clear to you that there's no truth in the stories the newspapers are running about me.'

'Oh, I see,' said John, and his relief was evident.

'I felt I had to see you to get things straight between us,' Freddie went on. 'Do you remember anything at all about the time we spent together when you were small?'

'Not really,' replied John, visibly relaxing a little. 'Although I do vaguely remember being in Blackpool with you – when would that have been?'

Freddie filled him in with a few dates, although he was careful not to mention the tragic circumstances of their parting. Before long the tension had dissipated and soon they were enjoying a laugh or two over some of Freddie's reminiscences of his childhood. After about ten minutes they parted with a handshake, John apparently satisfied that Freddie wished him no embarrassment and Freddie happy to return to his chosen routine. The great reunion was over – it certainly hadn't been disastrous but neither had it been a mind blowing success.

Later John confided to his friend Pete Shotton that he had instinctively liked his father on that first meeting and had been delighted to find that he was just as crazy and eccentric as he was himself. Nevertheless he did nothing to follow things up at this time. He had been raised with the preconception that his father had abandoned him as a baby and, however much he would have liked to move closer to Freddie, his lack of trust and subconscious bitterness prevented him from doing so.

Freddie now accepted what appeared to be an interesting vacancy in the famous Skindles Hotel near Maidenhead, but he had hardly settled in before the press resumed their relentless pressure. He did try his hardest to dodge them, but they were well supported in their efforts by members of the staff and Freddie found himself being constantly waylaid. On one such occasion he threw his apron over his head in an attempt to elude the photographers, much to the fury of a reporter from the *Daily Express*.

'You're going to regret this,' he burst out in his frustration. 'Even the Royal Family don't dare deny us pictures. If you try to avoid us you'll be sorry – you'll be bloody sorry.'

It was true that the less he complied with the press, the more derogatory were the stories they printed about him. It seemed that he was good copy and the name Lennon sold newspapers. He thought back to the advice of his friend on the *Sketch* who had arranged the meeting with John.

'They're going to write articles about you whether you like it or not,' he had explained. 'You'd do better to give your story to a ghost writer and get the true facts across. It would be easier than trying to avoid the newspapers – and you'd get paid for it too.'

He finally decided that it was only by talking that he stood any chance of shutting them up, and so he sold his story to *Tit Bits* for the princely sum of £200. The money allowed him to enjoy the first holiday he had had since his schooldays and also to replenish his wardrobe. But after a month or so of living in hotels instead of working in them, he was more than ready to begin grafting again.

He thought a job away from London for the winter would enable him to lose his identity once and for all. And besides, so he thought, the Beatles couldn't stay at the top forever. He was wrong on both counts, of course. Nevertheless he managed to settle down to work in a hotel in Shepperton where although everyone knew of his relationship with John, it was finally accepted with the indifference he preferred it to be. At last he was able to talk about the Beatles like everyone else without feeling embarrassed or being asked for his autograph. That is, until the day he met Tony Cartwright.

A few doors down from the hotel there was a club where the chef had introduced Freddie as a member, and it was here that Freddie met Tony one evening. Freddie was off work on sick leave and had called in for a pick-me-up to prepare himself for a visit from the doctor the next morning. Tony was working as Tom Jones's road manager at the time under the supervision of Gordon Mills, and had dropped in with Tom on their way home.

Somebody must have mentioned the fact that Freddie was John Lennon's father, because Tony came across to talk to him and casually to introduce himself. At that moment Freddie was singing with the rest of the customers to a guitar and drums duo who were providing the entertainment, and Tony seemed impressed with his voice.

'You're pretty good Scouse,' he commented. 'No need to ask where John got his talent from. Have you ever done anything yourself in the showbiz line?'

'I've been an entertainer all my life, Tony,' smiled Freddie. 'Although I never made the big time – by choice or by fate, I guess. But I pride myself on having made a lot of people happy in my time.'

'You used to work on the ships, didn't you?' Tony questioned him further. 'I read the story about you in *Tit Bits.*'

113

'I used to organize the ships' concerts and do a bit of singing – I still do when I get a chance.'

After the sing-song Tony took Freddie over to Tom Jones's table where the singer was enjoying a drink with a group of friends. Tom was beginning to be recognized at the time and his record 'It's Not Unusual' had just entered the charts. No embarrassing comments were made, and when they left Freddie assumed it would be the last time he was likely to see them again. And even Tony's 'See you, la' – he was also from Liverpool – he accepted as final.

For this reason he was somewhat surprised to bump into Tony again a few nights later at the club. Freddie had slipped in for a nightcap at about eleven o'clock, and the place was by now almost empty. The two boys who had been entertaining on the previous occasion were idly strumming out a few numbers and a party of four were at the bar.

It was then that he saw Tony stretched out on one of the divans, obviously dozing off, but as Freddie went across to him he jumped up excitedly.

'Hello, la,' he roared. 'I've been waiting for you.'

Not for one moment could Freddie imagine why, and he had to wait patiently before finding out while Tony went over to order drinks.

'How about making a record? I'll be your manager,' he finally blurted out all in one breath.

Freddie had, of course, liked Tony from the moment they first met. To start with they were both Scousers, and in many ways Tony reminded him of a younger version of himself. Young and full of drive, he shared the same irrepressible spirit and sense of humour as Freddie, although he was definitely far more ambitious and his sights were aimed squarely at the top. But for the life of himself Freddie just couldn't share Tony's enthusiasm about launching him into the world of pop.

'You're fucking crazy,' he laughed, convinced that he must surely be joking.

114

Tony, however, was deadly serious and didn't stop talking for a good ten minutes as he tried to convince Freddie that he had nothing to lose.

'Your voice is bloody good and I've got a group called the Loving Kind that'll give you the perfect back-up. You've got a lot of talent, you know, la,' he enthused.

'Don't bullshit me, Tony,' replied Freddie. 'The real reason you want me is because I'm John Lennon's father, isn't it?'

'Well, the name Lennon is going to help,' added Tony cautiously. 'And with your ability you'd be mad not to take advantage of it.'

'That may be what you think, but as far as I'm concerned it's precisely for that reason that I'm just not interested.' And that was the end of that as far as Freddie was concerned.

But once again fate intervened, bringing Tony and Freddie into a closer relationship and causing Freddie to see the situation in a slightly different way.

One of the two entertainers, who had been paying a lot of attention to them, suddenly came across and addressed himself to Tony.

'Is little fancy pants trying to move in on the Beatle scene?' he taunted.

For all of his size and well-built physique one would hardly have classed Tony as a fighter, but James Bond himself couldn't have made a more devastating response to the nasty innuendo. In a flash his indolent form sprang from the divan and his well-aimed right-hander literally slung his tormenter across the room. Another fantastic leap carried him headlong to the platform where he grabbed the legs of the other musician, which brought forth a number of inarticulate curses.

A loud yell of 'Run for it, Freddie!' was the first indication that Freddie was involved, and for some unknown reason he answered the call and followed the

115

fleet-footed Tony from the club.

On arrival at the hotel where Freddie worked, Tony's demands for shelter from his pursuers resulted in a noisy argument with the night porter, who summoned the new and highly indignant young manager to the scene.

'You're waking up the whole hotel,' he fumed, and on seeing Freddie out of his sick bed at this unearthly hour of the night he registered his displeasure in no mean terms.

'You can collect your bloody cards at the end of the week – that is, if you haven't pegged it,' he sarcastically informed him.

By this time the pursuers had found the place of refuge and their loud taunts of 'Come out, you yellow bastard!' eventually woke the residents from their sweet repose. For a moment Freddie thought the distraught manager was about to throw Tony and himself into the arms of the howling predators, but he boldly went out and warned them he would ring for the police if they didn't buzz off. Tony delayed his departure for as long as possible and left Freddie with the comforting words that he would see him early the next morning.

It is doubtful whether Tony went to bed at all that night, because he was in Freddie's room before nine o'clock the following day.

'Come on, get dressed. We're going to London,' he raved as he made short work of the cold bacon and egg which Freddie's companion in the kitchen had brought to him.

Freddie gave him what he assumed was a wan smile. 'Some other time, old chap,' he answered feebly, sinking back against his pillows. But Tony was not to be daunted in his aspirations for the 'star-to-be' and he whipped the blankets off from the bed, exposing Freddie's nudity to the early morning draughts.

There seemed to be little point in resisting. He had lost his job, would soon be homeless and felt much too weak to argue. So, having collected his few possessions, he followed

Tony languidly to a waiting van which looked as if it was about to fall to pieces. No one appeared to have witnessed their departure and when the doctor called later and received no reply he ordered the door to be broken down, fearing the worst. On a much later visit for his cards, Freddie was handed a bill for damages from the manager of the hotel and another from the owner of the club.

On the hazardous journey to London Tony attempted to encourage his shivering companion with words of comfort. 'Just you wait till we've signed the contract, la,' he enthused. 'I'll get you all the Harley Street specialists you want and a private ward full of cracking nurses to tend to your every need.'

With surprising alacrity Tony was indeed successful in arranging an interview with someone of importance at Pye Records, and, having assured one and all that they were writing their own number, he was given the go-ahead and invited to return in a couple of weeks for a recording.

They were fast reaching the point of no return, and Freddie was only too aware that he would need to reach a rapid decision about the whole crazy business. It was years since life had been such a laugh, and his unquenchable appetite for fun tempted him to go straight ahead.

He did of course wonder what John would think of the escapade and was hopeful that Tony's reassurance that it could only make John proud of his Dad would prove to be right. But in the end it was his inability to turn down an opportunity for adventure which caused him to take the bull by the horns and to throw himself whole-heartedly into the mad turmoil of the pop business.

The next couple of weeks were something of a nightmare, the first and most important step being to write the promised song.

'All we need,' said Tony cheerfully, 'is enough money for a flat and a car.' This was easier said than done, the only possible source of help being Freddie's brother Charlie. But when Freddie mentioned that Charlie lived in Solihull, Tony was inspired by another brilliant flash.

'The Loving Kind have three engagements in the Midlands this weekend,' he announced. 'So all we have to do is to go up with them in the van and pop in to see Charlie.'

The trip in fact proved to be most successful. During the journey they managed to finish writing the song, a kind of condensed story of Freddie's past, gloriously entitled 'That's My Life'. Charlie was duly impressed, and as a future investment in their potential he subscribed the handsome sum of £200, which Tony used to buy a car.

They celebrated their success with a gigantic meal, the first they had had for some time. Back in London Tony even found them sleeping quarters with a friend in Richmond, the only drawback being that they had to sneak in after eleven o'clock and out again before seven in the morning to escape the wrath of the landlady.

All they now needed was a song for the flip side, but Tony had that wrapped up too. With Gordon's introduction they went to Leeds Music where Freddie met Don Agness, the only man he learned to respect in the pop business apart from Gordon Mills. Don was more than prepared to help, but solemnly warned him of the pitfalls that lay ahead for the novice.

'Trust no one in this business,' he advised him. 'And always get a contract checked out before signing it – there are a lot of sharks around.'

He suggested that one of Vera Lynn's old numbers entitled 'The Next Time You Feel Important' might be the right type of song for Freddie to sing, and it was the words rather than the music which led him to accept the proposal.

On the great day of the recording Don himself was present, surprisingly accompanied by Gordon Mills, and quite a few other people who were strangers to Freddie were sitting in the box above the studio. It was about eight in the evening when Freddie started recording, and he was warned that the session might continue for five or six hours.

'There's no way I can sing for five hours unless you provide me with some lubrication,' he threatened his young manager.

'It's more than my life's worth if they see us bringing booze in here,' was Tony's apologetic answer, but they overcame the obstacle by buying half a dozen small 'dragons' bloods' (very strong beer) which Freddie managed to conceal in his pockets.

Freddie was somewhat astounded by the size of his back-up – not only the Loving Kind but a dozen or more session men and not least the lovely Ladybirds. After various scales and what not he was escorted, by now feeling distinctly nervous, to a three-sided cubicle, where the only people visible to him were the boxed brigade above.

Tony came to the mike in an endeavour to cheer Freddie up and/or to stop him drinking the dragons' bloods, but he was unaware that the mike was switched on and that everything he said could be heard. And as he pointed to a well-formed blonde in the box and remarked, 'I wouldn't mind a session with her', his words resounded right round the studio. The blonde happened to be the recording manager's wife and she shot out of the box in high indignation, making some very pointed observations about Scousers and demanding an apology. Freddie managed to knock back two more dragons' bloods before peace was declared, and Gordon decided to remain with him to save Tony any more embarrassment.

'The Next Time You Feel Important' – and Freddie felt anything but – was to be the first number to be recorded, as they thought it would take longer than the 'masterpiece'. The biggest problem was Freddie's tendency actively to demonstrate his emotions as he would normally do in front of an audience.

'You're not singing a bloody opera,' chastised Gordon. 'You've got to keep still for the mike.'

Nevertheless it was finished by ten, whereupon they carried straight on with the 'easy one'. It was about one o'clock before he was finally through, feeling extremely winded and parched. Everyone appeared to be quite happy with the session, but Freddie felt somewhat disappointed.

'It would have sounded better if Gordon had let me show some feeling instead of standing there like a stuffed dummy,' he complained to Tony. 'As it is, I reckon I could have done better by myself in a phone booth.'

There then began the important operation of 'selling Freddie', as Tony put it. It was one mad round of visiting joints they couldn't afford but expected to soon, and Tony's devious ways of gaining admission presented them with some difficult problems, particularly on the night they gained entrance to the Scotch Club via the back stairs. Freddie was in deep conversation with pop singer Peter Noone when a whispered voice interrupted him: 'It has come to our attention that you are not a member, sir, and would sir care to join his manager on the pavement outside,' breathed the baby-faced bouncer with menacing gentility.

It was essential to create the right 'image', which necessitated the purchase of some new gear and a certain amount of sprucing up. Freddie had of course sported long hair for years, and with the addition of a snazzy leather waistcoat he quickly looked the part. As Tony so often affectionately taunted him, he was quite simply 'the oldest teenager in the world'.

He did make a feeble protest when Tony announced that they had an appointment with Tom Jones's dentist where he was to receive the 'smile of the century'. 'Where the hell do you think we can get the money?' demanded Freddie, gritting the few teeth the dentist had left him.

'Don't worry, it'll only be about £20 at the most,' responded his ever-optimistic manager – although the final bill was £100 and Freddie was hounded for two years by the 'royal dentist' for payment.

However, they did manage to have some happy times, notably in a pub called the Anchor off the beaten track in Shepperton, run very ably by a manager and wife who had had previous experience behind the footlights. One particular evening Tom Jones brought his father along and he and Freddie light-heartedly discussed the possibility of launching a group called the Fab Fifties.

The first big break was an invitation to Amsterdam to sing the record on TV there, which meant, however, that Freddie had to learn the song in Dutch. Amsterdam was good fun, but once more things nearly went disastrously wrong. Although Freddie had practically mastered the Dutch words, they had assumed that he would only have to mime the song, with the words placed in a strategic position for him to see from the mike. But precisely fifteen minutes before they were due on the air, Tony burst into the dressing room in a state of panic.

'It's bad news, la. You're going to have to sing live – do you think you'll be OK?'

Miming had already been banned in Europe and the show was to be broadcast live to a packed audience, a sort of chat show affair in which the stars were called on and interviewed. Fortunately Freddie's past experience with ship's concerts saw him through the ordeal and he felt very proud on coming out of the studio to find a mass of screaming teenagers fighting for his autograph.

'Bloody hell – you've made it, Fred!' gasped Tony. 'Some of them even want you to autograph their arse!' And to Freddie's utter astonishment, distraught girls were baring all parts of their anatomy to receive the much sought after signature.

The next day was hilarious. They felt that Amsterdam belonged to them and Tony played his role perfectly, protecting and promoting Freddie simultaneously, assured that they were certain to make the grade. Even Freddie himself began to believe they might be in with a chance when, on the morning of the record's release, it was charted thirty-six on the radio. And in an attempt to buy a copy himself he found that the shops had sold out on the first day. The following morning it charted number twenty-seven and Gordon Mills himself commented: 'It looks pretty promising.'

But then the inexplicable happened, and the next day the record disappeared completely from the charts. It just didn't seem to make sense. Tom Jones, just back from Europe, told Freddie he'd heard his record being played there more often than his own. And when Tom arrived in America, news seeped through that it was going like a bomb in nine states and had actually topped the charts of three. Yet it seemed the record was dead in Britain.

On visiting Pye to enquire about the unaccountable news, Tony found that his questions were simply ignored at every level. But he was on friendly terms with one of the secretaries, who took him discreetly to one side. 'It was Brian Epstein who blocked the record,' she confided. Brian Epstein was of course the Beatles' manager.

Freddie was not only astounded at this news but furious, and his immediate reaction was to try to contact John. It wasn't that he blamed John for the withdrawal of the record – he simply hoped to enlist his help in intervening with EMI on his behalf. But when he and Tony called at John's house in Weybridge at eleven o'clock one evening, John didn't make them feel particularly welcome.

'Fuck off,' was his short but far from sweet greeting as he slammed the door in his father's face. He had no intention of speaking to Freddie in the presence of Tony Cartwright, whom he mistakenly believed had come to 'make trouble'.

John's reactions to his Pop's 'pop' venture were actually rather mixed. He had been angered by Freddie's story to *Tit Bits* and was basically opposed to any of his relatives or

122

friends 'blabbing to the press'. Part of the reason for this was his fear that Mimi might be upset by the revelations. But he also resented the idea of his Dad – or anyone else for that matter – muscling in on his name.

Nevertheless he bought a copy of Freddie's record and it was played regularly at Kenwood, his spacious home in Weybridge. John's son Julian, who was then just three years old was especially fascinated by the record and repeatedly asked his mother, Cynthia, to 'put on Granddad's song'. It gave John a secret thrill to think that his Dad was a 'real character' with some talent in his own right, but he was still too suspicious of Freddie to trust him or openly to acknowledge his interest in him as his father.

Having considered the bad news more reasonably, Tony decided to ask the young secretary for a written statement which might possibly enable them to take legal action. But when they arrived at the Pye studios the next day they discovered that the girl in question had been conveniently promoted to a 'far better' position in Los Angeles. Their suspicions were confirmed by Tom Jones on his arrival back from America.

'You've had it, whacker,' he informed Freddie. 'They told me in the LA studio that your record had been withdrawn without explanation.'

Disillusionment was no stranger to Freddie, but he was unfamiliar with the cut-throat dealings of the pop industry and felt very shocked by the sudden turn of events. In fact it was the realization that he was powerless to do anything about the situation that led him to resolve to quit, and he dealt Tony quite a blow when he informed him that he was 'retiring back to a world of human beings.'

He visited the catering agency and took the first live-in KP job available, which happened to be at the Toby Jug Hotel, Tolworth, Surrey. And it was here that, for once, fate proved to have a more joyful experience in store for him.

6
AN EXTRAORDINARY ROMANCE

The Toby Jug Hotel was on my home territory, although I had never actually visited the pub, or any other pub for that matter, until that unforgettable Christmas of 1966, some six months after my eighteenth birthday. It was rather unusual for me, but I felt a sudden urge to take a vacation job that winter to provide me with a little pin money during my first year at Exeter University. And at the suggestion of my friendly Irish neighbour Maura, who ran the local off-licence, I plucked up courage to give the Toby Jug a ring.

'They're always looking for helpers over the Christmas season' she advised me.

It was on the very first day of my glass-washing duties that I made the acquaintance of Freddie Lennon. He himself had begun work at the pub only a couple of months previously, but already he had made himself completely at home. In fact he was singing loudly and throatily, much to the delight of the kitchen staff, when I first caught sight of him standing at the sink up to his elbows in suds.

He was an extraordinary figure, short but of a stocky, muscular build, with long black hair, greying slightly, swept back somewhat theatrically behind his ears. But perhaps the clothes he was wearing were the most striking thing about him: bright red trousers and a yellow tee-shirt, topped by a black leather waistcoat – not the usual sort of gear for one of his generation, I thought.

It was nevertheless extremely difficult to ascertain just how old he actually was – middle-aged for sure, but his face was curiously free of wrinkles or frown lines and his eyes sparkled with sheer zest for life and, I suspected, a somewhat wicked sense of humour. He was constantly spouting all kinds of witticisms and wise-cracks, mainly addressed to the chef, and I freely admit that I was fascinated at first sight.

For his part, Freddie's first view of me was from the rear as I washed wine glasses for the following session. He felt an instant urge to get to know me, and as if his thoughts had been transmitted to me I turned around and smiled at him. My face seemed curiously familiar to him, as though we were meeting for the umpteenth rather than the first time, and he experienced an uncanny elation.

My hopes of making his acquaintance were rewarded at about three o'clock in the afternoon when he sauntered over, wiping his hands on his greasy apron, and enquired whether I would like a cup of tea. 'Yes, please,' I beamed unhesitatingly, and I doubt whether I could have felt more delighted if he had invited me to a champagne reception.

As we sat at the huge wooden table, where he was soon to begin peeling spuds for the evening menu, I was totally oblivious to my unceremonious surroundings. The chat was mainly small talk, but it was not the content of the conversation that seemed important. It was as if I was speaking to a great friend from whom I had been parted for many moons but with whom I immediately felt relaxed and comfortable.

'Do you mind if I call you Polly?' he asked as we parted. 'It was my mother's name, you know, and somehow or other you remind me of her.'

Later that afternoon as I walked towards my home I felt myself to be floating on air. It seemed as if something of tremendous importance had occurred, although I wasn't sure what, and my thoughts centred excitedly on the following day and the possibility of developing our friendship.

That next afternoon we took a stroll through the

surrounding countryside and our conversation touched on much deeper subjects than before. To our mutual amazement we found ourselves discussing politics, religion, the deep mysteries of life.

'I haven't talked like this with anyone for years,' remarked Freddie, to which I replied that I didn't think it possible to feel so close to anyone so quickly. From the start we were totally open with each other – it seemed rather wonderful.

It was later on, when I was about to leave for home, that Freddie handed me a couple of Christmas cards, addressed and stamped, and asked me to post them for him on my way. My eyes nearly popped out of my head when I saw that one of the cards was addressed to John Lennon at his home in St George's Hill, Weybridge.

'Yes, John Lennon is my son,' announced Freddie, noting my surprise. 'We're not really in touch, but I always send him a card at Christmas.'

It seemed fairly obvious that he intended me to discover his identity, but despite my fascination I felt a tinge of disappointment that he had revealed his secret so soon. From now on he might be nagged by doubts as to whether my interest was in him or his name. And so might I.

I made directly for the off-licence, bursting to tell Maura about my new and infamous friend.

'Oh, did I not tell you that Freddie Lennon worked at the Toby Jug?' she winked impishly. 'They say he's a lovely man, a widower you know, his wife was knocked down and killed by a motor car. But it's a terrible shame the way his son treats him, him a millionaire and his poor father working as a kitchen porter.'

My interest in Freddie was deepened by my instinctive concern for the underdog, and I actually became quite preoccupied with the injustice of his lot. I knew nothing of John's background – having little interest in the Beatles –

but I imagined he must be quite inhuman totally to ignore his own father.

'You mustn't judge John so,' was Freddie's response to my indignation when I raised the matter the following day. 'He thinks I walked out on him when he was a kiddie and then turned up again when he made the grade. Although it wasn't like that at all – I loved his mother desperately, and little John, and I'd have still been with her to this day if she hadn't left me for another man.'

'Was your wife very beautiful, then?' I asked quietly, struck by the tragic romanticism of the situation.

'Julia was as beautiful as a summer's day – long red hair and a gorgeous figure. I loved her with all my heart, and of course I still do. In fact I've never loved anyone since.'

I couldn't help but feel somewhat inadequate in the face of such adulation, and as the first pangs of jealousy struck me I realized with surprise that my infatuation was deepening.

Fortunately it was soon time for me to pack my bags for Exeter – a chance, I told myself, to shake off this folly and return to the company of boys of my own age. But it was when we were saying our goodbyes that I astounded myself even further. As I gently touched his cheek with a little kiss I found myself whispering the words 'I love you', although I certainly hadn't intended to say them and they echoed mockingly in my ears. I knew at once from his look of cynical disbelief that he didn't believe me, however much he would have liked to. And most definitely I didn't believe it myself.

I found out later that he just didn't dare to take our relationship seriously for fear of disappointment, although he repeatedly pestered the waitresses at the Toby Jug for advice and for their assessment of the situation.

'Do you really think it's possible for a younger girl to fall in love with an older man?' he would question them hopefully. Then the next minute he would pull himself together in an attempt to be realistic. 'I know how it'll be – a couple of letters and then she'll forget all about me.' And that of course is precisely how it happened.

But I found it impossible to forget Freddie Lennon for long. After a couple of months of dating immature lads I began to find their company boring and their conversation incredibly limited. Freddie had often described himself as a student of the 'university of life' and I found myself longing to listen again to his tales of the diversity of human nature. He was a fascinating and irresistible companion and it soon became clear to me that I had well and truly fallen under his spell.

I visited him again at the Toby Jug that Easter, where our love for each other blossomed in the distinctly unromantic setting of the hotel kitchen. And it was there, against a background of pots and pans and hapless carcasses hanging from hooks, that Freddie knelt on the sawdust floor and proposed.

'Marry me, Polly darling,' he pleaded, tears of sincerity glistening in his eyes. 'I've been waiting for you all my life and I love you so much.'

But it was not long before we were both laughing at the absurdity of the situation and we brought ourselves back down to earth with a cup of tea and a cigarette. Nevertheless his words had set me thinking deeply, and I began to question the future prospects of our relationship. With a thirty-five-year age gap I imagined that we would be seen as an extremely unconventional couple and that we might attract a certain amount of prejudice and criticism – and how right I was.

Strangely, it was not so much our relationship as such that people objected to as the suggestion that it was to be taken seriously or that it should be put on a permanent footing. It seemed that it was all right for us to have an affair – it was the idea of marriage that made people's hair stand on end. My friends at Exeter were constantly reassuring me that it was just a phase that I would soon outgrow.

'You've got to try to see it objectively,' they would urge me, eyeing me with pity and concern. 'It just couldn't work out with such an older man – you'd really regret it in a few years' time.'

The opposition from my family was also building up and my mother, Jean, was becoming increasingly concerned as she came to realize the depth of my feelings. My father had died two years previously – one of the reasons, I suppose, why I found Freddie's company so completely fulfilling – so that Jean felt it necessary to act especially protectively towards me.

'You see, I have to be both mother and father to her now,' she had explained to Freddie on the first occasion they met. 'And that's why I just can't agree to her continuing with such an unsuitable relationship.'

To an eighteen-year-old rebel like myself, such opposition was guaranteed to lead me to dig my heels in. Like Julia before me, I found respectability and convention one big turn-off, and the more my friends and relatives urged me to finish with Freddie the more desirable and exciting our friendship became.

Eventually I was left with just one loyal supporter, my dear friend Janet, who uttered no words of reproval and patiently listened to my tales of woe and indignation. And it was with Janet's help that I persuaded Freddie to pack in his job at the Toby Jug and try to find work in Exeter so that we could see more of each other.

Sadly, however, there was no work to be found, his money soon ran out, and to all intents and purposes he was back on the road again. In despair he even tried for a KP job at the university, but one look at his long hair and loud clothes convinced the bursar that he was little more than an overgrown student himself.

Neither did he have any luck at the university chapel,

which he visited one evening to find a night's repose. He was sleeping peacefully under the portals when he was gently awakened by the prod of a foot.

'Come along, my good man, this isn't a Sally,' announced the highly indignant clergyman in perfect Queen's English.

Finally, after he had spent the night at the railway siding in a goods carriage which transported him to the other side of town while he was asleep, we both had to admit that things just weren't working out. Inevitably we quarrelled, and I ended up losing my temper. So on my return from a lecture one afternoon I was hardly surprised to find a short note awaiting me under my door.

'My dearest Polly,' it began. 'It is quite obvious that one in my hopeless plight has absolutely no right to entertain the idea of marriage to a girl who has her whole life and career ahead of her. I love you Polly with all my heart, but I now know there can be no future for us together – PS I shall be working at the Greyhound Hotel, Hampton Court should you wish to contact me.' He obviously wasn't too concerned to keep his whereabouts secret!

I smiled somewhat ruefully at his letter, realizing that there was little alternative but to follow him to apologize for my hasty words. So it was with a certain amount of trepidation that I boarded the midnight bus for London and set out in search of the Greyhound Hotel.

I arrived, fraught and exhausted, well before breakfast time at Hampton Court – the location of the famous sixteenth-century palace which was the home of King Henry VIII. The village was more or less deserted, but I was fortunate enough to bump into an amiable-looking chef who was just leaving the staff quarters of the hotel to start his early morning duties, and who was more than delighted to help me with my enquiries.

'I'll take you straight to Freddie,' he smiled after I had told him the full story and explained who I was looking for. 'And if you love him don't allow anyone or anything to stop

130

you being together. I was in love once, but my girl died of leukaemia. We only had one year together.'

The chef's quiet words made a huge impact on me as I realized that the time Freddie and I would have together would inevitably be limited by our age difference. After all, he had already lived a large part of his life before I had even been born. And at the time of my birth in the summer of 1948 he was in fact awaiting execution in Buenos Aires under the mistaken identity of the South American murderer John Alennon.

We spent a blissful day wandering around Hampton Court Palace, and when I left once more for Exeter we swore that never again would we be parted. But this of course was much easier said than done, and the very first problem I faced was an upsetting confrontation with my mother.

'This ridiculous situation has gone on long enough,' she announced unrelentingly. 'I'm not prepared to allow you to see him any longer, so you'd better find a way of breaking it off. For goodness sake come to your senses, child, and see what a mess you're getting yourself into.'

It was really to escape the heat that I decided to find a temporary job in France where I could consider matters coolly and calmly without undue pressure. My mother was pushing me into making a stand about Freddie one way or the other. There seemed to be so much at stake, and I had to be certain my decision would be the right one.

'Don't worry, darling, this will be the final test,' I reassured Freddie as I set off for a post in Paris as tutor to two young children.

'Just remember I love you.' He waved cheerfully but with tears in his eyes, fearing once more that he would never see me again.

It was at this point that fate took a hand in the proceedings, for as it turned out the prestigious-sounding job failed to live up to my expectations. It seemed that in

131

addition to coaching *les enfants* my duties were also to include cooking, cleaning and general skivvying, which definitely broke the terms of my contract. I thought of looking for another post, but already the pangs of loneliness were making my heart ache for Freddie and it seemed quite insane to remain parted from him.

I visited my favourite church in Paris, the Sacré Coeur in Montmartre, hoping for a flash of inspiration, and after two hours of quiet contemplation before the Cross I felt I had my answer. 'You have the precious blessing of true love,' were the words that echoed in my mind, although a small voice seemed to be warning me that the road ahead would nevertheless be hard. But as I walked down the endless steps of the magnificent basilica I knew deep within me that we would surely receive all the help we ever needed, no matter what might befall us in the future.

Getting home was clearly to be the first of my difficulties, as I had received no wages and had no more than a few francs in my pocket. I despatched a desperate plea for help to Freddie, but judging on reflection that his assets were unlikely to be any greater than mine I decided against waiting for a reply.

Undeterred by Freddie's grim experiences with British consulates abroad, I boldly entered the Paris office and unapologetically demanded repatriation. To my surprise my request was instantly granted and I was loaned the wherewithal to buy my ticket home.

Twelve hours later I was back in London, secure in my newly made decision and looking forward to being reunited with my crazy and lovable friend. But destiny had been active in his life too, and unbeknown to me had resulted in a totally unexpected reconciliation between Freddie and his unpredictable son, John Lennon.

During the summer of 1967 a number of significant developments took place in John Lennon's life which were to have a direct bearing on his reunion with his father. During August he became interested in the mystical teachings of the Maharishi Mahesh Yogi, an Indian guru who was giving a series of lectures in London. At the instigation of George Harrison he learned to meditate and found that the peace and euphoria this discipline provided enabled him to kick his drugs habit. Meditation was to form the new 'high' in his life.

The spiritual teachings of the Maharishi also caused him to reassess many of his beliefs and values. He began to question bitter attitudes he had held for many years as he strove to model himself on the yogic ideal of perfect peace and love. Given that the first step towards discipleship is to learn to forgive one's parents, it was with some misgivings that he started to examine his feelings towards his father and his behaviour towards him since their meeting three years earlier.

Then, while John was meditating on these concepts, as chance would have it he received a most unexpected letter from his Uncle Charlie, his father's faithful and devoted younger brother. Charlie had been privately horrified by the unjustified attacks on Freddie's honour since John's rise to fame. And when he heard that John had actually slammed the door in his father's face on his recent visit to Weybridge, he felt the time had come to do something about the situation. So, without Freddie's knowledge, he had written to his nephew in his usual outspoken and straightforward way, exonerating his brother and explaining the true facts about the break-up of his marriage to Julia.

'It's about time you stopped listening to lies about your father and understood that it was not his fault that his marriage broke up,' he angrily demanded of John. 'Any man coming home from sea to find his wife pregnant by another man would have had a right to ask for a divorce, but your father forgave your mother and took her back. Despite all that she ended up by walking out on him for someone else – and she took you with her. There are two sides to every story, John, and I would suggest that you forget everything your aunts have told you about your parents. Now that you are a grown man, why not invite your father into your home, talk to him man to man and make up your own mind about him.'

To John the letter was a complete shock and something of a revelation. As yet he had been given no details whatsoever of the split between his parents, except for Mimi's hints that his father had been a bad lot. This was the first intimation he had received that it was his mother who had been the 'guilty party', and he felt compelled to raise the matter with Mimi, albeit with considerable anxiety and hesitation.

As ever loyally defensive of her favourite sister, Mimi's explanation was brief and non-committal. It was true that Julia had 'made a mistake' while Freddie was away in the war, but she really didn't wish to discuss the matter further. Curiously afraid of upsetting his strong-willed aunt, John let the matter rest there, although his eyes had been opened to a previously unknown aspect of his childhood. And in particular he had begun to view his father in a new light.

But it was probably the death of Brian Epstein from a drugs overdose on the night of Saturday, 26 August 1967 that represented the most important trigger to John's reconciliation with his father. With Brian's departure from his life John had lost a powerful father-figure, a man who had adored him, believed in him, even idolized him in a way his natural father had never been able to. A void now opened up in John, giving rise to a longing to replace the steadfast paternal support he had received so liberally from Brian.

Thus it was without hesitation that John, on receipt of a short note from Freddie offering his sympathy on Brian's death, finally decided to take the initiative to bridge the gulf between himself and his father. Just six days after Epstein's death, John put pen to paper and addressed the following letter to Freddie at the Greyhound Hotel:

> Kenwood
> Cavendish Road
> Weybridge
> Surrey

Dear Alf, Fred, Dad, Pater whatever,

It's the first of your letters I've read without feeling strange –
so here I am answering it – OK? As you know I'm pretty tied
up at the moment, there's a hell of a lot to do. If I get time
I'll give Uncle? Charlie a ring, but anyway, I'll get in touch
with YOU before a month has passed. After that I'm going
to India for a couple of months so I'll try and make sure we
meet before then.

I know it will be a bit awkward when we first meet and
maybe for a few meetings, but there's hope for us yet. I'm
glad you didn't land yourself with a bloody big family – it's
put me off seeing you a little more. I've enough family to last
me a few life times. Write if you feel like.
Love John

PS Don't spread it (press I mean). I don't want Mimi
cracking up!

Mischievously aware of the impact his letter was likely to
have on his father, he scribbled the words 'Guess Who?' on
the back of the envelope. He was always one to exploit to the
full the emotional hold he had over others.

It was at about this time that the first 'authorized' biography
of the Beatles had been commissioned, which was to be
written by Hunter Davies for Heinemann. John wanted the
book to give a true and unadulterated history of his life, and
realized that his reunion with Freddie provided an excellent
opportunity to include his father's side of events and to
portray a balanced account of his childhood. So he duly
despatched the author to Hampton Court to interrogate

Freddie about just what had happened during his early childhood years.

There was, of course, a bonus in the situation. John was utterly genuine in his desire to get to know his father, and the personable Hunter Davies, with his friendly, confidential manner, was just the man he needed to convince Freddie of his sincerity.

Freddie was only too happy to relate his own side of the story and he willingly provided Davies with a detailed description of his marriage to Julia and of the events leading up to their parting. In fact it was immediately after his interview with Davies that I returned unexpectedly from France and heard, for the first time, the extraordinary news of John's proffered hand of friendship.

'I'm sure John really means it, darling,' Freddie told me excitedly. 'He wants to clear my name in the biography. It seems I'm no longer to be the villain of the piece.' Unfortunately his hopes were unjustified, as unbeknown to us most of Freddie's material was later vetoed and the final text was to portray him, once again, as the archetypal scoundrel and ne'er-do-well.

John publicly admitted in 1971 that he allowed his Aunt Mimi to influence the manuscript in accordance with her own version of events. Neither of us had reckoned with the tremendously powerful influence which Mimi exerted over him. As mentioned by John in his first letter to Freddie, he was innately afraid of Mimi 'cracking up' and it seemed that the decision to edit Freddie's interview had been governed by his desire to protect her feelings. But Freddie was as yet unaware of the outcome of the book, and he looked forward with anticipation to the promised meeting with John.

It was actually about one month after the arrival of John's letter that Freddie received instructions from Weybridge that a car would meet him at Kingston Post Office at about two in the afternoon. He was sitting over a pint in the pub opposite, dithering with apprehension, when dead on two an unmistakable black limousine drew up. As Anthony, the chauffeur, briskly climbed out from the driving seat, Freddie crossed the road and was surprised to be recognized by a complete stranger.

'Hello, Freddie, this is for you,' announced Anthony, handing him a long envelope which crackled delightfully, revealing its contents. 'Jump in,' he urged him. 'We're going to Weybridge.'

For some unaccountable reason Freddie was almost paralysed by the thought of meeting John and found himself emphatically replying, 'No, I can't.' However, Anthony was not to be so easily denied and he instructed Freddie commandingly to get in the car for a minute.

'Look here,' he began in earnest tones, 'you're to keep the money, and you don't have to go to Weybridge if you don't want to. But I can tell you that John will be very disappointed if you don't, and as for yourself you'd be a bloody fool not to take the chance to meet him.' Freddie knew in his heart that the chauffeur was right, so having adjusted himself a little better to the idea he cheerfully gave in.

As Freddie confided in me later, he could hardly have described his arrival at Weybridge as particularly spectacular. John's house, Kenwood, was located on the St George's Hill private estate and was guarded by an electronically operated drawbridge-type gate, which scarcely gave Freddie the impression of home sweet home.

It seemed that the frontage of the house had deliberately been arranged to deter unwanted visitors. A fearsome poster of General Kitchener, forefinger pointing imperiously, had been positioned strategically behind the hall window, so that on dark nights it gave the appearance of a menacing bouncer. Immediately inside the entrance the guest was likely to stumble over a huge knight in armour who offered even less of a welcome.

Freddie was met by the unsmiling servant Dot, who

escorted him through a mirrored door into the living room. Here he was greeted by John's wife Cynthia, whose sweet concern, reminiscent of a typical homely Lancashire lass, at last allowed him to feel a little more comfortable.

It was about eleven o'clock that evening before John eventually arrived home from the recording studios. Freddie had been mentally rehearsing his greeting all day, but as John came towards him with his arms wide open, words seemed inappropriate. They enjoyed a long embrace, the first for more than twenty years, as John softly murmured: 'It's all over now, Dad, let's forget the past.'

Freddie's eyes were moist as, once again, he felt the warmth of his son's body against him, just as he had when John was a child. He felt a surge of remorse that so much time had been lost, but at least there was now a chance to put things on a new footing. And there could be no doubt whatsoever that both he and John were sincere in their desire to do just that.

They sat over a cup of tea, trying to put themselves at ease with each other, alone in the silent house apart from Cynthia and Julian who were upstairs in bed. John had already made up his mind that he wanted his father to live as one of the family, and lost no time in suggesting he should move in to Kenwood immediately.

'Tomorrow I want you to take Anthony with you and collect all your things. Tonight you'll be sleeping in the guest room, but after that you can take over the rooms in the attic – it'll be like your own place. What do you say, Fred?'

Not for one moment had Freddie imagined that he would become a permanent lodger at Weybridge, but he happily acquiesced, looking forward to the prospect of many long conversations with John. They were both too tired to talk much that evening, but resolved to have a proper chat the following day.

'We've loads to catch up on. See you in the morning, Fred,' was John's contented goodnight.

'See you in the morning, John,' replied Freddie, hardly believing that the events of the past day had really happened.

But there was little time for the promised heart-to-heart the following day . . . or the next. John did not usually rise before eleven o'clock in the morning, when he would come dashing down the stairs to eat a hurried breakfast, usually a plate of mushrooms on toast, promptly set before him by Dot or Cyn. The meal took him only as long as a quick glance through the morning mail allowed him, whereupon he would yell for Anthony to drive him up to town in the Rolls Royce. It was usually midnight or later before he returned after a hard day's night of recording, by which time Freddie was inevitably nodding off or had already tired of waiting and gone to bed.

It soon became obvious that he was to see very little indeed of John, who seemed totally preoccupied with the demands of his work. And on the rare occasions when he did have a few moments to share with his father he seemed fearful if not incapable of talking to him in any depth.

At least Freddie did have the chance to get to know young Julian, whose only previous acquaintance with his granddad had been through Freddie's record 'That's My Life'. But Julian's companionship was no substitute for adult conversation and as the days and weeks passed Freddie began to feel more and more alone in the huge, lifeless house. There was little that Cynthia could do to relieve his boredom, immersed as she was in her own round of social activities, and neither was there any company to be had from the few visitors who appeared spasmodically, worshipping at the shrine.

He attempted to walk to the local pub, where he was hopeful of finding a little companionship, but Weybridge was at least a mile away and, although he was a travelling man, he completely lost his way in the maze-like private estate. Dot, the housekeeper, did possess her own means of transport, but her supercilious expression warned him against attempting a closer relationship or asking for a lift to town.

It struck him as faintly amusing that John had seen fit to put his old Dad into retirement, assuming he would be delighted to idle away his remaining few years like a horse put out to grass. At other times he saw himself cast in the role of the 'mad' relative, to be confined to the attic regions away from public scrutiny, rather like Rochester's wife in *Jane Eyre*. It was totally against his nature to remain shut away from company for so long, and an overpowering sense of claustrophobia began to descend upon him.

But it was not until the appearance of Cynthia's rumbustious and plain-speaking mother, Mrs Lilian Powell, on one of her regular visits to Kenwood, that anyone recognized his restlessness.

'For heaven's sake, man, you look as frustrated as a hen in a coop,' she remarked one morning over breakfast in response to Freddie's god-forsaken expression. 'Why don't you get them to find you a flat where you can do your own thing?'

Freddie hesitantly agreed to consider the idea, his main worry being John's reaction, but before he had even had time to consider the question Lilian had already broached the matter with her son-in-law. And the speed with which she helped to implement the operation suggested to Freddie that it wasn't only the 'lodger' who was to be more comfortable after his eviction.

They found him a ground-floor flat in Kew, the only disadvantage being that it was necessary to cross the back yard in order to reach the bathroom from the bedroom. 'But at least it meant I was back in the world of the living,' he remarked to me later. 'I'd have gone crazy if they'd kept me in solitary confinement much longer.'

However, this restoration of freedom was marred by

John's disappointment at his leaving. Freddie had detected a look of dismay on his face as Cynthia informed him of the arrangements that had been made.

'OK, Dad,' he said, looking away. 'If that's what you want, I'll make sure you're fixed up with everything you need.'

But it was clear from his withdrawn attitude that he had not expected this turn of events. And Freddie learned later from John Francis, the part-time chauffeur, that John had been 'very upset indeed' about his father's departure. Nevertheless he gave orders to Dot to ensure that Freddie was given a couple of weeks' supply of food, and Cynthia went to great trouble to provide him with a carpet, a TV and some bedding for the new flat. He was also to receive a weekly allowance of £10, carefully assessed to correspond to the wages he had received as a KP – not a penny more – or less. This 'pocket money', promptly despatched each Friday by Bryce and Hamner, the Beatles' accountants, was intended to allow him to give up work, although in reality he was now worse off financially than when he had his live-in job as a KP. He now had to pay for his own food, which in the catering trade is 'all found'. Nevertheless, all in all he felt it was a kind gesture on John's part and he thanked him heartily for it.

'But there is just one thing, John,' he pointed out. 'You will make sure my insurance stamps are paid, won't you, or it will affect my entitlement to a pension.'

'Don't worry, Dad,' was John's reassuring reply. 'I'll get Apple to sort it all out. They'll look after everything for you now.'

Before Freddie actually left Kenwood he did find the chance to inform John about his friendship with me, a revelation which caused John a great deal of surprise and finally convinced him that his father was not quite as 'past it' as he had thought.

'So there's life in my old Dad yet,' laughed John with

141

more than a hint of admiration in his voice. 'You must bring her along to meet me.'

It was a relief to know that John approved of our relationship, as I was facing nothing but opposition from my own family. My mother had been angry at my return from France, knowing that it meant a resumption of my friendship with Freddie, and she was now firmly forbidding me to meet him or contact him, forcing me to arrange secret rendezvous in Kingston.

Nor was she the only person who was outraged by our love affair. Friends, neighbours and relatives alike felt that my relationship with a man of fifty-four was nothing other than scandalous. They were also intimating that my interest in Freddie was motivated by an infatuation with John, and that whether I realized it or not I was simply 'jumping on the band wagon'. I suppose I could have tried explaining that John Lennon in no way turned me on – I had always been a Rolling Stones fan – but logical argument was useless. The pressure upon me to give up Freddie was relentless, and my position at home was fast becoming intolerable.

I had already begun to suffer severe headaches and periodic blackouts when I received John's invitation to spend the weekend at Kenwood, so I welcomed the chance of a short break. I had arranged to meet Freddie at the Southampton Hotel in Surbiton, from where we would be driven to Weybridge by John Francis, the cabbie who worked part-time for Cynthia while Anthony was busy chauffeuring John around town.

As we sped towards Weybridge, it came to me with a jolt that most girls would have given anything to be in my place at that moment. There I was with the golden opportunity of meeting the number one Beatle, but I had been through so much of late that the impact of the situation was really lost on me. Nevertheless, during the journey I began to question

Freddie as to just what John was really like.

'Don't worry, pet, you've nothing to fear from John,' he assured me. 'I know he can be very aggressive, but I've seen his gentle side and believe me he's a nice guy.'

We arrived about midday and were met at the front door by Cynthia, dressed in a black sweater and red velvet slacks. Her reassuring smile and quiet charm made me feel reasonably relaxed.

'John isn't up yet,' she informed us, leading us through to the cosy little living room which opened off the kitchen and was actually the only spot in the vast house which in any way resembled home. We chatted a little about my predicament, and Dot made us some tea as we sat admiring John's huge collection of zany prints and lithographs which adorned the white walls, waiting for the entrance of the 'great one'. Cynthia seemed more in awe of John's imminent arrival than I was myself as she listened intently for his step on the stair with an expression of flushed anticipation. Finally her patience was rewarded.

'I think I can hear him now,' she breathed, glancing at me to check my reaction. I was soon to discover that John enjoyed an almost regal status at Kenwood, which he was encouraged to maintain by the demeanour of the household members and by his visiting friends. From that very first meeting I revolted against the courtier-like role and resolved to treat John as I would anyone else – even if it did mean foregoing his patronage.

My first sight of John as he entered the room certainly destroyed my preconceptions of the man. He appeared much more delicate and gentle than the solidly tough, macho image he projected on stage. Tall and surprisingly narrow-framed, he walked with an almost mincing shuffle – always in his stockinged feet – and it immediately struck me that there was something rather feminine about him when he was relaxed.

He didn't seem especially surprised to see me sitting at his

143

dining table, and after a casual greeting he began ferociously to attack the mushrooms on toast which constituted his usual breakfast. His table manners were the most atrocious I had ever witnessed. He said little, but as he munched I noticed him sizing me up with those penetratingly suspicious eyes that were to become quite familiar to me during my stay at Kenwood.

It was Freddie who broke the tension by drawing attention to John's tendency to squint when he wasn't wearing his granny glasses, which he had not yet put on for the day.

'He's as blind as a bat without his glasses – just like you, pet,' commented Freddie, referring to my own short-sightedness.

'I see you don't like wearing specs either,' smiled John. 'You know, when Cyn and I used to go to the cinema we were both too vain to wear our glasses so neither of us could see what the film was about.'

'And we couldn't hear it either,' chipped in Cynthia. 'If you're short-sighted it affects your hearing too, you know – you can't lip-read so well.'

The barriers between us now dissolved completely as we laughed and joked over our relative degrees of blindness, and for all his years Freddie was the only one amongst us who still had perfect sight.

'Well, John, what do you think of my Polly?' he finally asked, putting an arm around my shoulder. 'She reminds me a little of Julia. What do you say, John?'

I felt rather embarrassed to be compared with John's mother, especially when I caught sight of the uncomfortable expression on his face. But he dodged the question neatly, remarking that I reminded him more of Cyn. It was true that Cynthia and I did resemble each other a little, having the same long blonde hair and similar facial features. But it was immediately clear to me that John's mother occupied a very special place in his heart.

As my mind cast itself back to the last paragraph of John's first letter to Freddie – 'I'm glad you didn't land yourself with a bloody big family, it's put me off seeing you a little more' – I wondered what John's reaction would be should we decide actually to get married. He had clearly assumed that Freddie was still single, and hadn't reckoned on finding himself with a stepmother as well as a long-lost father.

However, it was soon time for John to leave for town, and we spent the rest of the day relaxing and playing with four-year-old Julian who was thrilled to see his granddad again.

When John returned home much later that evening we all sat watching TV in a cosy circle. The programme was a documentary about heroin addiction, and I distinctly remember the look of horror on John's face as the wretched junkies recounted their tales of degradation.

'It must be fucking terrible to end up like that,' commented John, at which Freddie and I guessed with relief that he hadn't yet started shooting heroin. We knew from a member of the staff that he had been heavily into LSD prior to his 'conversion' via the Maharishi, and that after he had decided to give up the habit a vast quantity of the stuff had been buried in the grounds of Kenwood. But at least he wasn't hooked on the really hard drugs, and we certainly hoped that he never would be.

I enjoyed a delicious sleep in one of the sumptuously furnished guest rooms, the best I had had for months, and the next morning John and Cynthia sat down with me to discuss the problem of my mother's opposition to my relationship with Freddie.

John was thoroughly indignant at the idea of any parent laying down the law to a girl of nineteen. 'Your mother must be out of her mind,' he remarked in disgusted tones. 'You can count on us to do anything we can to help.'

'Yes, and I think maybe we really can help,' added Cynthia, suddenly hitting on a brilliant idea. 'I've been thinking for some time of finding a mother's help. How would you like to come and live here and help me look after Julian – baby-sitting and that sort of thing? I'd pay you a small wage, you'd have your board and keep, and you'd be able to see Freddie whenever you wished.'

To me the suggestion appeared as absolutely god-sent, but it was clear from the cutting look that passed from John to Cynthia that he was not so enamoured with the idea, although it was not until later that I discovered exactly why not. Cyn had an active social life of her own and had been trying to persuade John for some time to engage a nanny for Julian, which would give her much more freedom. But as John was understandably against the idea of a substitute mother for his son, having himself been parted from Julia at the age of six, they had reached a state of deadlock.

Nothing more was said on the matter until later in the day, when it appeared that something of a compromise had been thrashed out. John was badly in need of secretarial help in handling the large amount of correspondence – mainly from fans – that arrived at Kenwood each morning. So I was to work for him as a sort of correspondence clerk and I would provide Cynthia with baby-sitting services, not nannying as such but just looking after Julian whenever she was out. That way both of them seemed happy.

My qualifications for both jobs were questionable, but there was no way that I could refuse such a golden opportunity. My mother seemed reasonably satisfied when I informed her of my plans, so I gathered together my belongings at home and ordered a cab to take me to Weybridge, ready to begin my exciting new post in the Lennon household.

7
THERE'S HOPE FOR US YET DAD

I moved into Kenwood at the end of October 1967 and was duly issued with my own shiny red, electronic entry card which enabled me to come and go much as I pleased. It was also announced that I was to begin driving lessons immediately, which would allow me to ferry Julian to and from school in the smart black Mini with smoked glass windows which Cynthia normally used. Secretly I was hopeful that I might even have a chance to drive John's psychedelic Rolls Royce, which, when not in use, stood parked in the grounds beside the painted gypsy wagon, John's other pride and joy.

John nobly paid off my £10 debt to Her Majesty's Government which I had incurred when seeking repatriation from France. At the same time he discharged Freddie's debt to the 'royal dentist', by whom he had been ceaselessly pursued for payment ever since he had received the 'smile of the century'.

It was truly a bizarre situation – shortly after Freddie's exit from Kenwood, here I was moving in! But although we would still have some distance to travel in order to see each other, at least I now had a reasonable amount of freedom.

I was quickly installed in the attic suite, occupied by Freddie before me. It consisted of a bedroom with wash handbasin opening into a small sitting room. Up here also was a large music room containing John's recording equipment where, to my amazement, several of the Beatles' much prized gold discs were strewn carelessly around as if forgotten. The music room also housed a huge collection of

147

records which I occasionally borrowed to play on my own small hi-fi. It was in this unpretentious studio, filled with musical equipment and mementoes, that John and Yoko Ono were to make love for the first time some six months later.

Additionally stored in the attic regions were a vast quantity of John's discarded clothes, most of them worn only once or twice. Cynthia was most insistent that Freddie should choose whichever items he wanted to supplement his own meagre wardrobe, but unfortunately he was a size or two smaller than his son!

Finally, the roof space itself housed the ubiquitous kittens which periodically emerged to run wild throughout the house soiling the top-quality carpeting with 'little accidents'. In fact, brown ammonia stains had completely ruined the luxurious black Wilton extending throughout the ground floor – which anyhow showed up every speck of dust. Surprisingly, however, nobody seemed in the least concerned.

'John adores the kittens,' Cynthia told me. 'He can't bear the thought of getting rid of even one of them, however much damage they do.' And of course there was no shortage of money for repairs.

It seemed that one of my household duties was to maintain the cleanliness of this totally impractical carpeting – an almost impossible task. And matters were further complicated by Dot's unwillingness to assign to me any of the work which normally came under her domain. I was soon to discover the fervour with which John's employees guarded their status in the household. Quite understandably, Dot was also unhappy that her two teenage children would lose their jobs as baby-sitters for Julian, so that on those occasions when Cynthia had asked me to 'sit', Dot's children often turned up for the evening just as they had always done, rendering my own position superfluous.

Dot was not the only person who was somewhat

concerned by my arrival at Kenwood. On answering the telephone while working on John's correspondence in the study one morning, I was surprised to be greeted by a shrill voice at the other end of the line.

'Who's *that*?' it demanded ungraciously, puzzled by my unfamiliar voice. 'Who *are* you?' it shouted, completely ignoring my introduction of myself. 'Put me through to John immediately.' I later discovered that the caller had been Mimi, and I couldn't help but smile at the thought of her reaction had Freddie himself answered the phone.

Most of my mornings were spent in the study endeavouring to operate the smart golfball typewriter on which I was to answer John's fanmail, requests for donations, charity appearances and so on. The majority of the fan letters were from girls asking John for advice on emotional problems – they assumed that as a writer of love songs he had all the answers. As John had neither the time nor the inclination to play the role of 'agony aunt', I undertook to answer some of the pleas for help. John solemnly read my replies each morning at breakfast before I sent them off. I was unable to discover whether he approved of my efforts or not, as he never commented one way or the other. He was always a man of few words.

My afternoons were usually spent out walking or reading quietly in my room, but the peace and quiet soon became rather oppressive and the loneliness of the vast house began to take its toll. I suppose it was the sheer size of Kenwood that was most forbidding. Apart from the large split-level kitchen and the adjoining living room, the ground floor included a huge dining room abutted by the lounge which led in turn to the study, the room where I spent most of my time. The main staircase led upstairs from the entrance hall, but a narrow spiral staircase also linked the kitchen to the upper floors.

When I found myself alone at Kenwood during the evenings, apart from young Julian who was tucked up in bed in his own room, I simply dreaded climbing this creepy spiral stairway for fear of what might leap out at me. The isolated setting of the house and the knowledge that it was a prime target for burglars only added to my dread, and the slightest creak or bump in the night was sufficient to set my heart racing.

John himself was acutely aware of the risk of burglary, and before he retired each night he made a point of personally checking that all the window locks were secure, paying particular attention to the large patio doors in the living room. Perhaps his anxiety was catching!

The nightly lock-up was a ritual John never omitted, no matter how late he returned home – which was usually very late. In fact he hardly spent any time at all at Kenwood, and the luxurious fittings, such as the huge TVs recessed into the fireplace of every room in the house, remained largely unused. On the few occasions when he did spend a day at home he was invariably to be found seated at his white psychedelic piano in the living room, vamping out rhythms in the creation of some new song.

Cynthia was also out a good deal, especially in the evenings, and I soon noticed with surprise how very little time she and John spent in each other's company. In fact such was the irregularity of their respective comings and goings that they had agreed that whoever came home last would sleep in the guest room so as not to disturb the other. The master bedroom, which they normally shared, was actually a vast room on the first floor housing a massive eight-foot double bed and a sunken bath at the far end, and it was here that John loved to lie in till late in the mornings.

I observed very few dialogues between John and Cynthia, and the only conversation which struck me as significant took place in the study when they were sharing a drink with Freddie and myself from the 'globe' cocktail cabinet. John, sprawled out unceremoniously across one of the plush velvet armchairs, was clearly in one of his uncompromising

150

moods. And when the discussion turned to diet, he announced bluntly to Cynthia 'You're getting pretty fat, aren't you?' The tone of the comment was far from jocular, and the recriminating glance which Cynthia threw back at him confirmed to Freddie and myself that things were far from good between them.

But in spite of the isolation Cynthia seemed contented and her daily routine was well organized. She was still meditating – a legacy from the Maharishi – and claimed that it was only by meditation that she was able to withstand the pressures she inevitably faced as the wife of a superstar. It certainly must have worked for her as she was always a very calm and serene woman.

Boredom was her main enemy, but this she dispelled by outings on the town, often in the company of George Harrison's wife Pattie. These she seemed to enjoy immensley, and the following morning she would girlishly relate the happenings of the previous night to Dot, seated on the vast bed listening avidly. Dot played the perfect confidante, always ready to lend a willing ear or to cheer Cynthia up when she was depressed, and the two of them got on extremely well. However, it was the question of Cynthia's evenings out with the girls which brought about a rift between John and Freddie and led to John blowing his top with his father for the first but not the last time.

During one of my weekend visits to Freddie in Kew we bumped into Cynthia in a nightclub one Saturday evening. Whether it was due to an excess of alcohol or simply the prompting of old-fashioned values I'm not sure, but Freddie was deeply shocked to find John's wife clubbing without a suitable escort and he treated her to a lecture on the subject of wifely duties. It was one of the few occasions when I was really mad with Freddie. I knew he had a terrible habit of saying the most outrageous things under the influence of whisky, but I was furious with him for offending Cynthia.

I realized with despair that he had gone much too far, but

what I did not realize was that certain members of John's entourage who were also present in the club would report his words to John in a totally contorted form. In fact several different versions of the truth reached John's ears – the most ridiculous of which being that Freddie had attempted to seduce his daughter-in-law! The accusations were nevertheless sufficient to enrage John, and without waiting to verify their validity he paid an impromptu visit to Kew the next morning, *en route* for London in his Rolls.

We were enjoying a welcome lie-in when we were woken from our slumbers by a loud, not-to-be-denied banging on the front door. We were greeted by an extremely irate John.

'What the fucking hell have you been doing?' he thundered, not waiting for an answer. 'If you can't learn to keep your bloody mouth shut, the feud between us will be on again and we'll see what Fleet Street makes of that.' With these words he turned and stormed back to his limousine, leaving us both bewildered and totally helpless to retaliate.

Fortunately, on my return to Kenwood, I was able to acquaint him with the true facts which he was presumably able to confirm from other sources, and he sent a conciliatory message via me to his father.

'Tell him to forget the whole damn business and that I'm sorry I blew my top,' he instructed me. 'But warn him to keep that mouth of his shut – or else.'

John found another way of proffering the hand of peace by phoning his Dad one Sunday with an invitation to a fancy dress ball which was being held to mark the release of *The Magical Mystery Tour* and which was to take place on 21 December 1967 at the Royal Lancaster Hotel.

'You can wear what you like, but make sure it's a laugh,' were John's orders.

'I've got it, I'll go as a dustman,' exclaimed Freddie with sudden inspiration. 'Then you can tell all your friends "My Old Man's a Dustman".'

'Typical of you,' rejoined John. 'It should be bloody great.'

Freddie entered into the spirit of the occasion with his usual enthusiasm and completed his costume by carrying an old dustbin lid emblazoned with the words 'My Old Man's a Dustman'.

The selection of my own outfit was a little more of a problem. Lacking funds to hire anything more grand, I decided the only answer was to go dressed as a schoolgirl in my somewhat outgrown but still wearable gymslip.

It was when I returned to Weybridge the following day to root out my old school uniform, which I kept in my trunk, that I came across John lounging around the living room. We found ourselves unexpectedly alone in the house, giving us the chance for a heart-to-heart chat – or the nearest thing to it that I ever experienced with John.

'So how are things, then?' began John, which immediately astonished me as he had never been particularly talkative before.

'Everything's OK between Freddie and myself,' I ventured. 'But there's still a lot of pressure on me to break it off.'

'Have you made your mind up what you're going to do?' he asked.

'Oh, I definitely want to get married,' was my unwavering reply. 'I can't explain why, but I just know it's the right thing for me.'

'OK, but you know what you'll be letting yourself in for if you do get married, don't you? Everywhere you go you'll have people staring at you and pointing at you because of what you've done. Yes, for the rest of your life you'll have people talking about you. It won't be easy.'

In retrospect I realized that his fatherly advice must have been based on personal experience, but at the time I was not in the mood to pay it much attention.

'Look, John, I love him,' I explained. 'And I just know

153

that our story's going to have a happy ending.' From the expression on John's face I knew that he found it hard to believe me.

'You know your trouble, you're just a dreamer,' he said, bringing me down to earth. Rather an ironic comment, I thought afterwards, from the man who was later to write 'Imagine'.

'Are you telling me you don't believe in love?' I asked incredulously, thinking of the profusion of love songs he had penned in the past.

'Sure, I believe in love,' he reassured me. 'And I believe that love can break down all barriers.'

'Look,' he went on, getting up and beginning to stroll up and down as if the subject meant a lot to him. 'I'm really glad that you and Fred are together. For one thing it means that I don't have to worry about him so much.'

It was good to know that John did worry a little, but it was not until the night of the fancy dress ball that I began to understand his true feelings for his father.

John had arrived dressed as a teddy boy complete with side burns and leather jacket, accompanied by Cynthia as the Fairy Godmother, and I couldn't help but notice that the costumes they had chosen clearly reflected their totally different personalities. The wine, food and music flowed unceasingly all evening, but shortly before the preview of the film, scheduled to be broadcast on TV five days later, on Boxing Night, something of a lull occurred in the proceedings.

John was seated at a large round table with Freddie and myself, together with Cilla Black and Lulu, amongst others. The anticipatory hush which had fallen upon the revellers as a huge screen was being erected was broken by a loud comment from one of the members of our table – Lulu, I think.

'Come on, John, why not do a number while we're waiting?'

'Not bloody likely,' he snapped, and then to my utter amazement he turned half-smiling to his father with the words, 'How about you, Fred?'

The atmosphere immediately became electric, and I sensed from John's apprehensive expression that he may have immediately regretted his suggestion. Instinctively he wanted to be proud of his father and to prove to the world that he was OK. But he had chosen a very public occasion to put Freddie's talents to the test, and if things had gone wrong he might have felt rather humiliated. And humiliation was not something John was used to handling.

For Freddie, John's invitation was probably the greatest dilemma of his life. Here was the golden opportunity to prove himself to John by showing that he was an entertainer in his own right. But should he fail to come up with the goods, it was likely he would cause John even more embarrassment.

As I glanced back and forth at the anxious faces of father and son I realized the tremendous tension that each was suffering. Fortunately or unfortunately, the problem was solved by the appearance of the master of ceremonies and the screening began of the ill-fated film that was later scorned by the critics.

The evening ended with a visit to a nightclub with Lulu and her BeeGee boyfriend Maurice Gibb, and it was not until the return journey home with just Cynthia and me that John and his father had a chance to discuss events.

But the evening had been a special one for both of them and it was not a time for mere words. Seated beside Freddie in the back of the Rolls, overcome by tiredness, John simply laid his head down on his father's lap and allowed himself to be stroked. Time seemed erased and, as naturally as though they had never parted, for a full thirty minutes Freddie caressed the back of his son's neck. As I observed father and son at last sharing a little of the love they had lost so many years before a lump rose in my throat.

155

Perhaps if Freddie had been travelling on to Weybridge John could have talked out some of the hurt he had been carrying with him for two decades. But the spell was broken when the Rolls stopped at our flat in Kew and it was not until a few days later, over the Christmas holiday, that John and Freddie were able to settle down to a really meaningful conversation.

It was one of the happiest Christmases that Freddie could recall. In fact it was the first Christmas he could remember ever having spent together with John, such was the amount of time he had been away at sea. On Christmas Day they exchanged presents, and Freddie was especially touched to receive a cigarette lighter, bought for him by young Julian out of his pocket money. It was a gift which remained one of his most treasured possessions until the very end.

The magic of Christmas and the prevailing spirit of peace seemed to nurture the sense of closeness which John and his father desired, and by the evening of Christmas Day John felt sufficiently relaxed to broach the topic of Charlie's letter.

'I've been meaning to talk to you about what Uncle Charlie said in his letter,' began John tentatively, as he and Freddie were enjoying a quiet beer together. 'He mentioned that you weren't to blame when you and Julia split up.'

'It's true that she left me for another man,' explained Freddie. 'But I suppose I must also have been to blame for driving her into his arms.' He chose his words carefully, grateful for the opportunity to set the record straight. But he was careful not to make recriminations against Julia, realizing how much John had idolized her and not wishing to add to his distress.

'But why didn't you ever come back to see me?' asked John with genuine curiosity.

'Pride, John,' replied Freddie. 'I've often reflected on what I've had to pay in my life for my obsession with pride

156

and principle. And the biggest price I paid was losing you.'

It seemed to John that Freddie's words held the key to the enigma of the past, but although part of him longed to know more, something held him back from pressing his father further, and he deftly turned the conversation to a more light-hearted note.

'It's one hell of a laugh that you and me Mum got married in the same register office as Cyn and I,' he smiled. 'Followed by a chicken dinner in the Big House over the road, eh?'

'You know something, John,' ventured Freddie, pouring himself another beer. 'I reckon you and I have got a lot in common. All my life I've despised the trappings of bourgeois respectability and the sickening hypocrisy it breeds. I always thought you felt the same until you accepted a bloody MBE and really let the side down.'

'Yeh – well, the less said about that the better,' mumbled John, noting that his father's attitude was the total reverse to that of his Aunt Mimi, who had declared John's decoration to be the greatest honour of her life.

'So you reckon I'm a chip off the old block, eh, Dad?' teased John, slumping further back into his armchair and focussing his gaze squarely upon his father.

'I always reckoned I could put over a song OK,' returned Freddie, breaking into a grin. 'And so did your Granddad, so I guess it runs in the family.'

The talk turned to music, and having learned with surprise that his father was something of a connoisseur with a wide knowledge of opera, John coyly enquired which of his own compositions was Freddie's favourite.

'I think all your songs are bloody great, if you must know,' conceded Freddie. 'But I've always had a special affection for "Penny Lane". It reminded me so much of my childhood – all the Bluecoat boys used to be sent to get their hair cut at Mr Bioletti's barber's shop.'

They spent the rest of the evening laughing and joking

about their mutual reminiscences of Liverpool, but the mood for any real confrontation had been lost. And so much that needed to be said once again remained unsaid.

The quietness of the festive season was soon over and for John it was back to an endless round of recording, appearances and business meetings. Freddie stayed on at Weybridge a little longer, hopeful of catching some more time with his son, but even when John was at home he was rarely alone.

John's off-duty evenings were usually spent on the floor of the lounge, smoking pot and listening to records, flanked by admiring cronies. Sitting in on one of these pot-smoking sessions, Freddie was struck by the hero worship John seemed to inspire in his friends and gained the impression that John was simply holding court. He found it impossible to talk to John in the presence of these 'worshippers at the shrine', and failed to understand why John did not surround himself with companions more on his own level. Relating to others as equals, and the open sharing of feelings that this demanded, appeared to be very difficult for John at this time.

One of my own duties at Kenwood was of course to care for young Julian, and I soon noticed with interest that he was very like his father in the way he related to his friends. Julian was already manifesting leadership qualities and asserting himself as boss amongst his peers. There was no shortage of young visitors from the 'top people's' estate falling over themselves to come to Kenwood to play with Lennon Junior. But despite his popularity he felt no compulsion to be 'nice' to his pals and thought nothing of telling them to get lost when he tired of them.

Unfortunately this same outspokenness extended to his mother, whom he would often answer back in the most impudent way, much to my embarrassment. Cynthia seemed untroubled by this, but there was no way that I was prepared to accept so much rudeness from a child of five.

The matter came to a head one afternoon when I was minding Julian in the lounge and in response to some directive of mine he spat out the words 'Shut up.' I smacked him sharply on the bottom at the very moment at which Cynthia entered the room, and it was clear from her expression that she was far from pleased with my action.

However, except when it went too far, I found Julian's lively spirit quite enchanting and enjoyed a lot of fun with him during the weeks I spent at Weybridge. First thing each morning he would come bounding up the stairs to my room on the top floor and would leap on to my bed to wake me up. After a game or two he would insist on my helping him to get dressed and together we would choose a suitable outfit for the day from the large collection of clothes in his room.

But despite the good times with Julian, there was very little for me to do at Weybridge. The fact that I couldn't type meant that I was really unsuitable to be the secretary John really needed. I could have continued to help Dot with the housework, but my career ambitions caused me to feel dissatisfied with a post as an au pair. It was decided by mutual agreement that I would bid John and Cyn farewell after the festive season, and having spent Christmas at home I returned to Kenwood only once more, in order to collect my belongings.

On my return home I found that my relationship with my mother was even more fraught. She was still refusing permission for me to marry Freddie, and, seeing my determination, she became very angry with what she considered my unwillingness to 'see sense'. I was beginning to consider whether I should look for other accommodation when my mother issued me with an ultimatum which finally made up my mind for me.

'I don't want you living in this house while you're seeing that man,' she announced on New Year's Eve.

I phoned Freddie in desperation to explain my predicament, but his warm comforting voice left me in no doubt as to my next course of action.

'Come home, Polly darling,' was his simple message, from which I knew instinctively that from now on my home would indeed be with him.

The next day I was on the move once again, and although I felt sad to be leaving home under such unhappy circumstances I was relieved that my future was finally decided. It was not until later that I realized that through her ultimatum my mother had possibly forced my hand. At the time it just felt good to be asserting my own independence, and at least I would no longer have to lie.

Comparing myself to the girl in John's song 'She's Leaving Home', I left a brief note which did not state my destination and called a car hire firm which John and Cynthia frequently used. As he helped me to unload all my worldly possessions at Freddie's flat in Kew, the driver was quick to put two and two together. And unbeknown to Freddie and myself, he later informed my mother of my whereabouts.

Now that we had finally set up home together, the idea occurred to Freddie and me that it would be simply wonderful to have a baby. We loved each other so much that it seemed the most natural thing in the world. And of course we were also aware that my pregnancy might pressure my mother into giving her consent to our marriage.

I was already nearly two months pregnant when a sharp rap on the front door at eight o'clock one morning announced the arrival of a lawyer's clerk who cheerfully served me with a summons. As I tried to digest the incomprehensible legal jargon, a sense of panic and despair began to beset me. My mother had applied to have me declared a ward of court, and if her action was successful the judge could well impose an order forbidding Freddie to contact me in any way, under threat of jail.

It struck me as utterly ridiculous that a woman of nearly

twenty could be subjected to such treatment. I had become used to the general disapproval of my relationship with Freddie, but it was now implied that there was something criminal about our liaison. I felt sickened by shock and bewilderment.

For her part, my mother had felt compelled to try to stop me from making what she believed to be the biggest mistake of my life. She saw no possibility of our marriage proving successful and was afraid that I would be irredeemably damaged by the experience.

The events of the next few days overtook me with frightening alacrity, and a sense of unreality prevented me from fully registering everything that happened. The afternoon before the court case I began to suffer severe abdominal cramps, and by the evening I had lost our baby. With my emotions as they were, the poor creature hadn't stood a chance.

A locum signed a medical certificate confirming that I was unfit to appear in court the following day, so mercifully I was spared the ordeal of standing in the dock as punishment for my love. Of course there was still the anxiety that we might be legally prohibited from seeing each other. But as John had placed at our disposal the services of David Jacobs, the top showbiz lawyer, now deceased, at least we were certain that our case would be well represented.

As I lay in bed on the day of the hearing, waiting for Freddie to return with news of the judge's pronouncement, my mind raced wildly, trying to imagine how I could possibly survive if the judgement went against me. Fortunately my suffering was rewarded: the judge saw no reason why we should not continue with our relationship, although he decreed we should not marry until I reached the age of twenty-one, which gave us some sixteen months still to wait.

However, my ordeal was not yet over as the question of publicity was now to impose further stress. At the application of our lawyers the ward of court proceedings had in fact

161

been conducted in closed court, denying the news-hungry reporters who hung around the London courts access to a bloody good story. And thanks to the *savoir faire* of David Jacobs, Freddie had been skilfully smuggled in and out through the back entrance of the court. The mere sight of his face would have been sufficient to set the Fleet Street bloodhounds relentlessly on our trail.

But although we were successful for some time in avoiding the attentions of the press, it was inevitable that sooner or later the story would break, and so it did. As John Lennon's father, Freddie still made front page news and the story of his 'scandalous' relationship with a young girl of nineteen was hot.

An unexpected visit from Don Short, pop correspondent on the *Daily Mirror*, sent me scuttling for cover in the coat cupboard where I crouched out of sight as Freddie nonchalantly fenced the reporter's probing questions. However, it was clear that we could no longer continue to dodge the press indefinitely, and the story eventually broke on the front page of the *Mirror*.

Just as John had predicted, everyone was talking about us and I began to understand the meaning behind his warning. It now seemed that I was an object of curiosity to be discussed in whispers, and several times Freddie was accused to his face of being a baby-snatcher. Our only friend was the old man who ran the corner shop, who appeared genuinely delighted for us and treated us rather like an indulgent uncle. But on the whole, London felt cold and disapproving, and the sense that we were now a public spectacle began to detract from the happiness that was rightfully ours.

There seemed little alternative but to move out of London, and flicking through the *Evening Standard* one evening we came across an advert for flats to rent in Brighton. As the rent was no more expensive than that of the flat in Kew, John's accountants sanctioned the move and we bid goodbye to London.

We moved into the tiny one-bedroomed flat at the end of April 1968 and began a brand-new life together on the south coast. At last, thank goodness, the future promised to be fun.

John Lennon's interest in the teachings of the Maharishi Mahesh Yogi had continued into 1968, and in February that year he left for India to spend two months studying spiritual matters under the guidance of his guru. Initially the trip proved successful and we received a picture postcard from him bearing the cheerful message: 'It's great here, hope it's great there.'

But it was during this stay in the Himalayas that John's respect for the Maharishi turned to contempt, and he eventually left India declaring that the Maharishi was a sham and had 'made a fool of everyone'.

Almost simultaneously with John's disillusionment with his spiritual teacher he began his extraordinary and deeply intense relationship with Yoko Ono, and from the time of his return to England she was the new mentor in his life. Yoko was seven years older than him, and her wide knowledge of culture and the arts supplied him with the kind of intellectual stimulation he had been lacking in his companions for so long.

The magnetic attraction that Yoko Ono was to develop for John was linked to the fact that she embodied, at one and the same time, traits of the two most influential women in his life. Her bizarre approach to art and fascination with the unusual mirrored the unconventional personality of his mother Julia, herself a non-conformist throughout her life. Yet her iron determination and emotional strength were more reflective of the strong-willed Aunt Mimi. And like Mimi she was to exert a tremendous emotional hold over John.

By the time we moved into our flat in Brighton, John had

already made love to Yoko for the first time in the attic regions of Kenwood. And although John was saying nothing at the time, his marriage to Cynthia was well and truly on the rocks. His letter to us expressing regret over my recent miscarriage gave no hint of the dramatic events which were taking place in his own life, and the only suggestion that anything unusual was happening was the fact that he had changed his phone number, always a sure sign that a new wave of publicity was imminent.

Wonderful Weybridge

Dear Freddie and Pauline,

Got the letter – sorry to hear about the baby – but glad to hear you're both happy. There's nothing much to say really – India was good – but glad to get back to work. Would love to come and visit you both – Julian digs the seaside. Give me a ring when you're plugged in – watch your arse in Brighton – loads of queers! Anyway write if you feel like.
With love John

New phone no. Weybridge 47776
This paper's a drag to write on

In fact it was not until we rang the Weybridge number and spoke to an extremely agitated Cynthia that we had any indication that something was amiss. Our suspicions were confirmed by the subsequent announcements in the press, but John himself never personally spoke to us of his relationship with Yoko, nor did we get to meet her until some two years later.

During those two years John was to become estranged from many people who had played an important part in his life until then, including Paul McCartney and various members of the Apple team. The rumour in circulation was that Yoko was attempting to cut John off from his links with the past, that she wanted him all to herself.

'It sounds like a bloody rerun of the story of John and

Mimi,' was Freddie's caustic comment.

The next communication we received from John was a scribbled note offering to pay our expenses for three weeks in Scotland, where we intended to elope in order to finally tie the knot.

In June 1968 I had discovered to my delight that I was pregnant once more, so that the need to make things legal became pressing. However, we were still under the jurisdiction of the courts and the smallest leak to the press might have alerted my mother to our intentions, enabling her to obtain an injunction to prevent us marrying. Secrecy was obviously of the utmost importance, and when we confided our predicament to John he graciously offered to 'arrange things' for us:

> Dear Freddie and Pauline,
>
> Sorry I never seem to have any time for you – anyway I know you understand. So – OK go to Scotland for three weeks and get married! Good Luck. Should I get P. Brown [a chief executive at Apple] to ring you anyway to arrange things for you? – I will, so wait for his call – It will probably be the day you get this letter.
> Lots of love, John   X
>
> Good luck.

The enthusiastic tone of the letter and the unexpected kiss gave Freddie and me the strong feeling that John had gained a new understanding and compassion for our plight by virtue of his own unconventional relationship. It was as though he was trying to share around a little of his own happiness.

We spent three crazy weeks in the motherly care of an Irish landlady in Edinburgh, who nursed me through my morning sickness with Scottish toddies and Celtic charm. The legal side of the proceedings was handled by a firm of Edinburgh lawyers who were entrusted with the delicate task of arranging for the banns to be displayed in the least public of places in the city in an attempt to avoid unwelcome press attention. We were well looked after by a kindly lawyer's clerk who assuaged our fears of discovery by organizing varied outings and activities for us. For some reason he was deeply touched by the tragi-comic story of Freddie, the prodigal father who returns to find his long-lost son has become an international idol. And he very nearly had us crying into our whisky glasses as he wryly commented, with all the eloquence of an advocate, on the pathos of the situation.

We managed to maintain our cover until the appointed day of the wedding, which by coincidence happened to be my twentieth birthday, and to our relief the ceremony proceeded without a hitch. Two passers by were summoned to act as witnesses, and there was a spirit of lunacy about the whole procedure which was reminiscent of Freddie's marriage to Julia so many years previously.

We returned to Brighton with a sense of triumph, and our darling son was born the following year at the end of February. We called him David Henry so he could drop the 'Lennon' surname completely later on, should he wish to disclaim any relationship to John. David's birth marked the beginning of an important new phase in Freddie's life; it gave him a second chance at fatherhood and allowed him to redress the mistakes he had made when John was a child.

Whereas he had spent very little time with John, he now took on the role of both Daddy and Mummy to David, whilst I went out to work to help supplement John's allowance. We must have been one of the first couples to engage in role swapping, but to us it seemed the most obvious course of action. Not only was I ambitious to develop a career in my own right, but I was also in a position to earn a higher salary than Freddie, whose age and lack of qualifications were hardly in his favour.

With his KP background he made the perfect house-husband, equally at ease with the housework, the cooking or changing nappies. Although he had been a moderate to heavy drinker all his life, he no longer felt the desire for alcohol and was largely teetotal from David's birth onwards. His new-found radiance seemed to confirm the truth of his comment that he had never been happier in his life, and there was no doubt that David was the apple of his eye.

'You're going to spoil that kid of ours if you make much more of a fuss of him,' I would laughingly complain.

'Listen, pet, you don't know how much it means to me to have the chance to be an indulgent Daddy,' he would reply. And I knew from the tears of joy in his eyes that he was somehow working out his redemption.

Things seemed to be almost perfect, and to crown our delight John bought a little house in Brighton in his father's name to allow us the extra space we now needed. Curiously, however, John showed no interest whatsoever in his half-brother, and his letters to us stopped abruptly not long after David's birth. But our happiness was such that we were not unduly concerned by John's silence, and neither of us had a care in the world until a book arrived in the post one morning.

It was Hunter Davies's long-awaited biography of the Beatles, but to our amazement the promised vindication of Freddie's good name was absent. Worse, the detailed interview which Freddie had given to Hunter Davies had been savagely cut, and much of the first chapter succeeded in depicting Freddie as a braggart and a rotter. His immediate reaction was total shock at the bitter realization that he had been badly let down.

Feeling sick with anger, we spent several days pondering the matter. Our main fury was directed at the author, whom we erroneously considered responsible for what amounted to character assassination.

'What the hell will my old shipmates – people like Jacko – think of me now?' fumed Freddie. 'And what sort of an impression will my kid have of me when he grows up and reads this?'

We contemplated taking legal advice, but Freddie was in a rather difficult position by virtue of his reconciliation with John.

'After all John's done for us, how in the name of Jesus can I take legal action against the book that he authorized?' anguished Freddie. 'I feel as if my hands are completely tied.'

The feeling of powerlessness was exacerbated by the guilt Freddie still felt towards John. He carried the burden of knowing that – albeit inadvertently – he had caused John suffering in the past, and he now felt incapable of stirring up any more trouble. Emotionally John had him exactly where he wanted him, and Freddie struggled to contain the feelings of disappointment and frustration with his son which now surged up inside him.

Ironically, Freddie was unaware that it was actually Mimi who had raised strong objections to his account of his relationship with Julia. By contradicting Freddie's side of the story and presenting him in the worst possible light, it was as if Mimi was finally releasing the torrent of rage she had felt towards him for so many years, a rage that had been based on the fear that he might suddenly appear and take her beloved John away from her.

In his interview with Jann Wenner in *Rolling Stone* in 1971, commenting on the Hunter Davies biography John claimed that his aunt had knocked out all the 'truth' about his childhood and his mother, and in allowing Mimi to do so he had effectively 'copped out'. Neither Freddie nor I had reckoned on the tremendously powerful hold which Mimi still exerted over John.

8
SO MUCH ANGER, SO MUCH PAIN

In the early summer of 1970 John Lennon was undergoing intensive treatment at the Janov Institute for Primal Therapy in Los Angeles. It was a hot day in June, but for some weeks now John had been isolated from the outside world, spending most of his time exclusively with his therapist, a highly trained, sympathetic man who had himself undergone primal therapy and with whom John had built up a high level of trust.

The session was being conducted in a small, sound-proof room without windows, the walls of which were padded on two sides to allow the patient readily to express the powerful emotions which would inevitably demand release. Audio and video recorders were in operation to provide a record of the session from which both patient and therapist could later gain useful insights.

But John was only minimally aware of his surroundings at the Institute. As he lay flat on his back on the floor, as was customary during primal sessions, his consciousness had returned to a day in June 1946, a day which had been so painful that he had attempted to blot it from his memory. But now, at the gentle insistence of the therapist, he began to recall every detail of the Saturday afternoon in Blackpool when, at the age of five and a half, he had been asked to choose between his parents but had finally ended up by losing both of them.

Slowly he began to tune into the atmosphere of the Hall's house in Ivy Avenue where he had been staying for some weeks with his father awaiting emigration to New Zealand.

It was here that Julia had unexpectedly appeared on that afternoon to ask that John be returned to her. The pungent odour of Freddie's Woodbine cigarettes suddenly filled his nostrils – he was once again sitting on his father's knee in the modestly furnished front room and his beautiful red-haired mother was standing opposite him, smiling at him with that irresistible smile of hers which always melted his heart. As he became aware of the haunting perfume she always wore, he recalled how much he loved her. But suddenly his father's voice interrupted the lovely warm feeling he was experiencing and the words he heard him speaking seemed strange and frightening.

'And what is your Daddy saying to you, John?' urged the therapist, noting John's distress but realizing the need to carry on.

John's reply was barely audible. 'He's saying "Mummy's going away and she won't be coming back again. Do you want to go with her or stay with me and go to New Zealand?".' He spoke these words in a whispered voice, drawing up his knees and clenching his fists with anxiety.

'I'm staying with my Daddy, I don't want to leave my Daddy,' John continued, but then he came to an abrupt halt and his features contorted as if he was now beset by some new unbearable fear.

'My Mummy's walking away down the road,' he recalled, speaking in increasingly shorter breaths. 'I'm running after her, I've reached her and I'm holding her hand. Daddy's still standing in the doorway and I'm shouting to him to join us. "Come on Daddy, come on Daddy," I'm shouting, but he won't come.'

The atmosphere in the session room reflected an electrifying degree of tension, and it was clear that John was experiencing a deep level of pain.

'Tell your father what you need of him,' instructed the therapist, encouraging John to follow through his pain and

170

to discharge the strong emotions which were now nearing the surface.

John found it almost impossible to give voice to the words he wanted to say, but they eventually came out in a choked sob. 'Daddy, I want you to come and join me and Mummy. I don't want you to leave me.' As he spoke it was as if he had suddenly released a floodgate of sorrow, and for the first time in many years his tears began to flow freely. But there was still more pain to be unleashed and it was the role of the therapist to push John a little further until he reached the core of his anguish.

'Your Daddy can't hear you, John,' he pressed him. 'Tell your Daddy what you need of him.'

'I need you to come after me. I need you to hold me, Daddy,' pleaded John, his voice now raised to screaming pitch as all the hurt and rage of nearly twenty-five years came pouring out. He was now on his knees, pounding the wall as he screamed the words 'Daddy, Daddy' over and over again. And as he punched away the pain, his feeling of anguish was compounded by a new and totally overwhelming terror.

His consciousness now shifted to the day he fell into a deep gully of sand on Blackpool beach, from which he was unable to free himself until his father found him. He felt himself to be surrounded by dark walls on all four sides and he was gripped by a sensation of blind panic as the sand appeared to be closing over him, shutting out the light of the sky.

'Daddy, Daddy, Daddy,' he screamed, his whole body now shaking with fear. But there was no way that John could make his Daddy hear him, and once again he felt isolated and deserted. He was overcome by a sense of dread that he would never see his father again.

It seemed that the trauma of the beach incident and the ordeal of his parents' parting a few days later had become

inextricably intertwined in John's subconscious, resulting in
an emotional burden which had remained with him since
childhood but which had been too terrible for him ever to
recall.

But now, as John curled himself into the foetal position,
the therapist knew that the worst of the tension had been
released, and at John's request he enacted the role of his
father and bent down to stroke his head gently.

It was only recently that Freddie himself had stroked
John's head in this way on the back seat of John's
psychedelic Rolls. The paternal caresses he had been denied
during his childhood now seemed to mean so much to him.

John Lennon's interest in primal therapy had begun in the
spring of 1970 while he was living with Yoko Ono at
Tittenhurst Park near Ascot in Surrey. He was sent a copy
of Arthur Janov's book *The Primal Scream*, which immediately made a deep impression on him and convinced
him that both he and Yoko could benefit tremendously from
this new form of psychological therapy. With his usual
enthusiasm and high ideals he threw himself whole-
heartedly into the treatment and spent the next six months
or so reliving and exorcising the emotional pain which he
had carried with him since he was a small boy.

Primal therapy is based on the notion that all neuroses
derive from childhood denials so intensely traumatic that
they cause us to block those of our feelings which are simply
too painful for us to handle. We thus develop powerful
defence systems which inhibit us from fully expressing our
whole selves and lead to greater or lesser degrees of
psychological stress and to physical diseases.

Arthur Janov's assertion that it is only by re-experiencing
the pain locked away in our subconscious that we can
become truly healthy and 'whole' made instant good sense
to John. The dichotomy of his aggressive, macho persona
and his gentle, easy-going inner self had interested him for

172

some time. He found it difficult to understand why he sometimes lashed out so cruelly at others when he knew in his heart that his ideals were those of love and peace.

He was also aware that his reactions were governed by admirably developed self-control. For years before Janov, he could never remember having shed a tear – not even when his beloved mother had been suddenly knocked down and killed. He had undergone more than his fair share of emotional suffering during his life, beginning with the shattering split between his parents and his resultant parting from both of them. Yet the more tragedies he was compelled to endure, and the more intense those tragedies became, the less he was actually able to 'feel'. By the time he met Arthur Janov in 1970 the emotional side of his nature was almost entirely shut off.

Perhaps the instant appeal of primal therapy stemmed from the fact that John was a natural psychologist at heart. He had an amazing ability to see through to the crux of any issue and, although a man of few words, was especially gifted at dispensing pungent home truths. Yet despite his talent in forcing others to confront their inadequacies he found it difficult to confront his own – that is until he began primal screaming.

Depending upon the particular emotions which have been blocked, primal therapy can result in the rediscovery of many different kinds of feeling. For John it was not only a question of reawakening his long-buried anger but also of learning to cry.

The tears which John shed over a period of many sessions with his therapist encompassed various aspects of the grief he had suffered during his childhood. Every sob, every scream was an expression of the torment he had experienced through the loss of his father, the loss of his mother and the sense of desertion which he associated with his parents' parting. To John it was as if he was actually feeling these pains for the first time. It was as if he had been released

173

from the grey twilight zone which had formed his reality for so long, and a brand-new world of many colours had opened up to him. There was no doubt in his mind that, for what it had given him, primal therapy was worth every cent of the many thousands of dollars he had spent on it.

It could well be true to say that primal therapy was the most formative experience of John Lennon's life. Although immensely demanding and painful – John compared the experience to that of being crucified – it proved supremely successful in freeing the feelings he had been denying for so many years.

And as a natural follow-up it unleashed a new outflowing of his creative talent based on the expression of those newly discovered feelings. The blandly sweet sentiments of the 'She Loves You' era were now long behind him as he embarked on a new phase in his musical career. His lyrics related more than ever before to himself and his own emotions. Not only had John found the courage to face himself, but he was also prepared to bare his soul to his public.

The most important artistic outcome of John's psychological therapy was probably the song 'Mother', a lament to the loss of his parents, written in the appropriately bleak solitude of Tittenhurst Park. The start of the song is marked by the sound of a church bell, a bell which John had frequently recalled during primal sessions as that of St Peter's church in Woolton, which he had heard for the first time on moving to Mimi's house after his parents' final separation. In his mind the cold metallic clanging of the church bell became associated with the sense of emptiness and rejection he was experiencing at that time.

However, there was another important outcome to the Janov therapy. An essential feature of the therapy consisted of the insights which patients gleaned at the end of good sessions, insights which could be helpful in triggering useful changes in their behaviour and their lives. By the time John

174

left California to return to Tittenhurst Park, he felt convinced of the need to express face-to-face with his parents the anger and grief they had caused him.

Although he felt no less fury towards his mother than he did towards his father, Julia was long dead and it was only Freddie to whom he had access. He realized it was essential to the healing process for him to speak to Freddie of his feelings about the past. And he finally came to the bitter conclusion that it would be an act of self-betrayal for him to continue to give financial assistance to the father from whom he himself had never received any support.

It was nearly two years since we had last been in contact with John, and with the advent of his thirtieth birthday the idea occurred to us to visit him to catch up on all the news. Freddie was particularly keen to discuss with John his plan to begin writing. For some time he had been feeling the urge to start work on his life story, and he was anxious to obtain John's approval and advice before he began.

We were actually very surprised when we received an instant response to our letter. A secretary at Apple phoned us almost immediately and confirmed that John would receive us at Tittenhurst Park, his mansion home near Ascot, on Friday, 9 October, the occasion of his thirtieth birthday. Little did we realize the reason behind his ready agreement to our visit.

We spent the two-hour car ride from Brighton excitedly discussing the long-awaited reunion and arrived at Tittenhurst around midday, looking forward to a celebration lunch. We had also brought a neatly wrapped birthday gift of aftershave lotion with greetings from Freddie, myself and eighteen-month-old David, who was to make the acquaintance of his famous elder brother for the very first time.

However, we had no sooner driven through the impressive entrance than our hopes of a harmonious meeting were shaken a little. The first person we saw coming out of the

175

servants' lodge was John's lumbering chauffeur Anthony, who had stayed with John since Kenwood days. But strangely he turned his head away from our shouted hello and continued on his way without acknowledging us.

We had driven only a few yards further towards the house when we were suddenly overtaken by a young girl driving a Mini, who abruptly enquired what our business was. On learning our identity she curtly ordered us to remain where we were and then entered the house, presumably to receive her orders. When eventually she returned, we were marched to the vast kitchen area where, feeling extremely bewildered, we were simply ordered to wait.

This unfriendly treatment was not the only reason for our sense of foreboding. The house itself appeared bleak and unwelcoming: the huge entrance hall was floored in icy white marble which gave the impression of a gloomy mausoleum, and the large rooms opening off it appeared strangely void of contents. Indeed, the only piece of furniture we noticed was a circular seat in the hall, which denied the occupants any possibility of eye-to-eye contact. I can remember thinking at the time that it seemed a bad omen for the prospects of our hoped for heart-to-heart.

In the kitchen, we sat at a large wooden table for some five minutes or so, nervously awaiting the arrival of our host, too tense even to talk between ourselves. The kitchen was the only room in the house which appeared to be lived in. Various macrobiotic foodstuffs were set out on the worktops, indicative of the special diet which John and Yoko were following at that time. We fidgeted uncomfortably, intrigued by the white spiral staircase which led up from the kitchen to the floor above. Only little David seemed capable of making himself at home as he played happily on the kitchen floor with the toys we had brought for him.

We were beginning to think that John had forgotten about our visit when he suddenly made his entrance, descending dramatically from the spiral staircase, closely followed by Yoko, and it was immediately apparent from their grim expressions that there was to be no question of a happy family chat.

The John we had known a couple of years ago was now unrecognizable. He sported a fiery red beard, reminiscent of his mother's colouring, which gave him the appearance of a fierce and primitive warrior and made our birthday gift of aftershave seem laughably inappropriate. His jaw was clenched with grim determination and behind his granny glasses the pupils of his eyes were contracted and staring. We had the impression that he was heavily stoned, maybe even on heroin which (in his *Rolling Stone* interview) he admitted to sniffing occasionally at that time when he was in 'real pain'.

'I'm cutting off your money and kicking you out of the house,' he snapped, stiffly taking a seat at the table and fixing Freddie with his penetrating gaze. This opening greeting set us reeling with shock, but before we had the chance to respond a sudden torrent of abuse poured forth from John, leaving us literally shaking.

'Get out of my life – get off my back,' he spat out in conclusion, raising his voice to an uncharacteristically high pitch as if he were trying to goad himself into a frenzy.

My initial reaction was that this must be some kind of sick joke, although it was clear from the look of sheer hatred in John's eyes that he was in fact deadly serious.

My glance turned to Yoko who was seated silently beside him, in the hope that she might be able to calm John down. But although I was struck by the serene beauty of her face with its flawless skin and perfectly proportioned features, her detached air and deliberately averted eyes left me in no doubt that she did not intend to intervene.

Finally finding his tongue, Freddie's reaction to John's words was quiet and faltering. 'All right, John,' he conceded. 'If that's your decision I accept it. But remember

I've never asked you for money – it was your choice to give me an allowance.'

These words seemed to act as a red flag before a bull, stirring John into a further furious outburst. 'Have you any idea of what I've been through because of you?' he yelled in crazed tones. 'Day after day in therapy, screaming for my Daddy, sobbing for you to come home. What did you care, away at sea all those years. . . .'

As his voice tailed off his rage seemed to change to anguish, and for one moment I thought he might even begin to cry. I felt genuine compassion for him and for the trauma I knew he had suffered as a child, but this was quickly replaced by a sense of indignation at the apparent unfairness of his attack on his father.

'You can't put all the blame on your Dad,' I protested. 'Your mother was just as much to blame for your problems.'

Astonishingly, the mention of Julia now triggered a vicious verbal attack on his mother, whom he reviled in the most obscene language I had ever heard, referring to her repeatedly as a 'whore'.

We were aghast. Neither of us could believe it possible that John could talk about his beloved mother in this way, and the horrifying thought struck us that Freddie's son was totally out of his mind, a suspicion seemingly confirmed by his following words.

'Look at me!' he screamed at his father. 'I'm bloody mad, insane. I'm due for an early death like Hendrix or Joplin, and it's all your fault.'

It was at this point that Yoko launched into a lecture on the seriousness of parental responsibility and the consequences to children in the event of their separation from their parents. It was a subject which may have caused her some personal concern – her own daughter, Kyoko, was living with her father, Tony Cox, and therefore she had only intermittent contact with the child. But before she had time to elaborate she was rudely interrupted by her unrelenting husband.

'Do you know what it does to a child to be asked to choose between his parents?' John roared. 'Do you know how it tears him apart, blows his bloody mind?'

I glanced at little David, still playing happily on the floor, apparently oblivious to the fearful atmosphere in the room and the blasphemies which flowed unchecked from his elder brother. As I thought of the purpose of our visit – to introduce John to our son – it seemed a cruel twist of fate that things had turned out like this. But as I reflected, John's outburst continued and the sordidness of his abuse increased still further.

'Father? You call yourself a father?' he sneered. 'You think that screwing some woman gives you the right to call yourself a father? You don't know the meaning of the word – you've treated me like shit, just like all the others. You've all ripped me off, the whole fucking lot of you.'

As if stunned by this self-admission, he fell back in his chair, temporarily exhausted, giving us the opportunity to try to collect our wits and decide how best to handle the situation. Noting that I was about to tackle John again, Freddie wisely whispered to me to say nothing. I could see from his worried glances towards David that he was beginning to feel fearful for all our safety.

'OK, John, I admit that I was partly to blame and I do understand your feelings,' acknowledged Freddie in un-characteristically subdued tones, hoping to calm John sufficiently to allow us to make our exit. But there was to be no possibility of escape yet, for John's aggression was simply rekindled by his father's acquiescence.

'How the hell can you possibly understand how I feel?' he demanded. 'How would you feel if you'd had nothing from your father all your life? How the hell do you think *he'd* feel?' he asked, pointing his finger furiously at little David who now began to cling to my legs, frightened by the growing violence in John's voice.

'Lock him away from his parents and ordinary human

beings and see how he'll end up – he'll end up a raving lunatic just like me.'

We were struck by the look of jealous rage which burned in his eyes as he glanced towards our son, a look which turned to pure hatred as Freddie anxiously picked up little David and hugged him closely to his breast, gripped by the sudden anxiety that John might even vent his anger on the child.

I now felt that I had taken as much as I possibly could, and despite Freddie's protests I was compelled to voice my indignation to John, although I knew in my heart that I was playing with fire.

'You've no right to treat your father this way,' I shouted, feeling genuinely incensed that we had been forced to endure such abuse.

It was clear from the despairing look that Freddie cast my way that he thought I was foolish to attempt to defend him, and sure enough my words seemed to inflame John's venom to a new and terrible pitch. Turning suddenly towards me, his furiously staring eyes burned right into me as his fist came crashing down on to the table in protest at my interruption.

'Mind your own business!' he screamed with deafening force in his voice, making a sudden move towards me which led me to fear that his verbal attack might easily progress into a physical one.

I caught the full impact of the powerful hatred which now came spewing out from John, and in spite of my determination to stand up to him my body began to shake with hysterical sobs.

My distress left Freddie in no doubt that neither of us could handle any more of John's rage. But as Freddie encircled me with his arm and made as if to rise, still clasping David tightly to him, John lurched forwards across the table and grabbed hold of Freddie's jacket lapel, confronting his father face-to-face.

'As for your life story, you're never to write *anything* without my approval,' he hissed. 'And if you tell anyone about what happened here today . . . I'll have you killed.' A look of sheer evil appeared on his face as he went on to explain in extraordinary detail the procedure by which he would arrange for his father to be shot.

'And do you know what I'll do then?' he taunted. 'I'll have you cased up in a box and dumped out at sea right in the middle of the ocean – twenty, fifty or perhaps you would prefer a hundred fathoms deep?' He spoke these words slowly and deliberately, as if he had been rehearsing them for a long time. And from the expression of malicious glee which lit up his face it was as if he was actually taking part in the murder as he spoke.

It was only in retrospect that I realized the significance of John's planned disposal of his father's body. It is not unusual, following psychotherapy, to experience a death wish towards a parent as part and parcel of the process of freeing oneself from childhood trauma. What was unusual in John's case was the method whereby he had visualized killing his father. By imagining him dumped deep in the ocean he was finally enacting his revenge on his father for the years he had spent at sea while he was a child.

As I turned in stunned horror towards Freddie I was struck by his sudden pallor and the expression of terror in his eyes.

'Come on, pet,' he whispered in an unfamiliar, empty voice. John hardly seemed to notice our departure and he remained sitting at the table staring fixedly in front of him, his eyes still alight with half-crazed anger.

Only Yoko arose as we moved silently towards the door. 'I'm sorry you have to leave this way,' she said – an incongruous attempt at civility uttered in her soft, bland, oriental voice.

Throughout John's tirade I had been aware of her remarkably powerful presence as she sat close beside him and in this respect I couldn't help but compare her with Mimi, herself a woman of powerful intensity. Although there the similarity ended, as Mimi was as narrow-minded in her attitudes as Yoko was outrageously avant-garde.

During the silent car ride home we each reflected gravely on the unbelievable events of the last hour. We were both suffering from a sense of unreality, as if we had lived through some terrible nightmare, and it was a good thirty minutes before either of us could actually find a voice.

'Don't worry, darling,' I tried to comfort Freddie. 'We'll soon put this awful day out of our minds. We'll forget that John ever existed.'

'I love you so much, pet,' replied Freddie softly, squeezing my hand. 'I know that while I've got you by my side I'll get by.' But despite his reassurances I felt I was powerless to relieve the torment he was suffering. The manner in which John Lennon had chosen to celebrate his thirtieth birthday was to remain stamped in Freddie's memory until the end of his life.

Over the next few days, as the shock gradually wore off, we found ourselves struggling to come to terms with the new situation. As I slowly assimilated the full significance of John's verbal attack, my sense of confusion gave way to feelings of fury with John and a tremendous sense of outrage on Freddie's behalf.

But to my surprise Freddie himself showed no sign of anger towards John. Instead he seemed to experience only an overwhelming guilt that his absence during John's childhood years had apparently resulted in immense psychological pain in his son, a pain we had witnessed first-hand and which appeared to border on violent insanity. If his assailant had been anyone other than his own child I am certain that his strongly developed sense of injustice would have led him to defend himself. But he seemed to feel totally powerless to reproach John in any way, and all his hurt remained locked away inside him.

By contrast, the confrontation with Freddie had allowed John finally to let out his own negative emotions which he had held towards his father – and to many others – for so long. For although primal therapy had laid the foundations of this emotional release, by expressing his anguish to Freddie face to face he believed he had furthered the healing process. Some of the energy he had previously channelled into fuelling his subconscious hatred and aggression could now be released in other directions.

The 'new' John was characterized by an almost frightening directness, and in the *Rolling Stone* interview with Jann Wenner published in January 1971 he finally spilled the beans on early Beatle depravity. There was no longer any need for him to project the image of the lovable mop-haired lad from Liverpool. John Lennon had begun the process of slaying his devils, and he felt himself closer to becoming his own master.

We hadn't really believed John when he had threatened to kick us out of our home. After all, the deeds were made out in Freddie's name and we had always understood that the house was to be his to live in for the rest of his life. But a few weeks after the hellish birthday party we received a letter from John's business manager demanding that we sign a deed of assignment transferring the property back to John. The tone of the letter was curt: we were to leave the house 'as soon as possible' or begin to pay John rent at the rate of £400 a year.

Also enclosed with the letter was Freddie's empty National Insurance card – not one stamp had been attached by Apple since the summer of 1967, despite the promises which had been made to him at the time. His contributions were now over three years in arrears, and unless we could find the money for the back payments his pension would be in jeopardy.

But despite our imminent homelessness, Freddie's main

183

worry was that John might actually carry out his dreadful threat of violence. Given John's present state of mind and the fact that he was a regular drug user, there was simply no way of predicting his likely future actions.

'Christ, pet, any day he could get half crazed on dope and decide he's going to have me shot and dropped into the middle of the ocean,' reflected Freddie, panic-stricken by the apparent ease with which his assassination could be accomplished. 'With his power, money and connections he'd have no trouble in hiring a hit man to get rid of me, and no one would ever be able to trace it back to him.'

I was alarmed by these words, and my knowledge of John's association with violent individuals such as the notorious Michael X, later to be hanged for murder in Trinidad, only added to my fear and anxiety.

But if I was highly nervous at this time, Freddie was even more distraught. His usual high spirits were permanently subdued and the sunny atmosphere of fun and laughter which usually filled our home was strangely absent. It appeared to be the notion of being dumped at sea which played most heavily on his mind and which he spoke of most frequently during the long, sleepless nights which he suffered for weeks after our meeting with John.

'I've never told you this before,' he confided to me one night as he paced restlessly up and down our bedroom. 'But I can't swim – daft for a sailor, I know – and all those years in the merchant navy I was secretly afraid of one day going down with the ship. I'm actually terrified of drowning.'

This painful admission at last seemed to release some of the emotion he had been holding back over the last month or so, and silent tears rolled down his cheeks as he sat ashen-faced on the bed. I was relieved that he was finally able to share the source of his fear, but it also struck me as uncanny that unwittingly John had chosen the most effective means of psychologically punishing his father. By planting in Freddie's mind the image of being buried at sea,

John Lennon had unknowingly unearthed his father's greatest phobia.

It was rapidly becoming obvious that we had little choice but to move from the house we were currently occupying. It was a three-storey town house which afforded excellent access to intruders, making us feel exceptionally insecure when we were asleep on the top floor. As Freddie's insomnia persisted we realized we needed to move to a new 'safe' address unknown to John, where we would feel less vulnerable. And as we had no intention of paying rent to our new landlord it was inevitable that we would have to leave the house sooner or later.

We were fortunate enough to find a smart two-bedroomed flat in a modern tower block on Brighton seafront which would be available in the new year. It was a comfortable little hide-away tucked up on the sixth floor, and the uniformed commissionaire who continuously guarded the entrance hall fostered our sense of security. The rent was just a little on the high side, but safe, cheerful surroundings were our highest priority at that time. And by an extraordinary stroke of fate our finances had recently received an unexpected boost by a fantastic win of £2500 on the football pools, which would obviously help us to meet the bills. Despite our misfortunes, we both had the feeling that somehow we were being 'looked after' by an unseen guardian angel.

But the problem of Freddie's terror of being shot and disposed of at sea still remained. Only once before had he feared for his life to this extent – way back in 1948 when he was awaiting execution under the mistaken identity of John Alennon – and again his son John had been indirectly implicated.

As the concern that John's threat might become a reality began to take a hold on Freddie, it was eventually decided that the ultimate answer was for him to confide his fears to a lawyer. So before we left the house he visited an old solicitor friend of mine with whom he lodged a detailed statement recording his recent conversation with John, with instructions that this statement should be made public if he should 'disappear or die an unnatural death'.

Not only did our visit to the solicitor serve to unburden Freddie of the fearful secret he had been forced to keep to himself for the last three months, but it was also an essential act of self-protection. It gave him at least a measure of assurance that John would be less likely to implement his threats now that they were legally on record. And from the alacrity with which John's solicitors reacted to the letter informing them that John's father's statement was now locked in our lawyer's vault, it appeared that Freddie's gesture of self-defence had indeed been successful.

John's business affairs were now represented by Allen Klein, who some two years previously had taken over the Apple organization, replacing many of the old faithful staff with his own men. Our negotiations were therefore on a different footing from how they had been in the old Apple days. No longer were we dealing with the affable and sophisticated Peter Brown, who had actually acted as godfather to our son. Peter Howard, the legal representative of ABKCO Industries, Klein's business management company, was a tough and uncompromising customer with no particular interest in our wellbeing, who seemed resolutely intent on implementing John's eviction orders.

We were therefore somewhat surprised when we heard from Mr Howard that John had agreed to our request to advance us £500, to be recouped from the later sale of the house, to help towards the fixtures and fittings for the flat. However, the loan was subject to some fairly stringent conditions. Naturally Freddie was expected to sign the deed of transfer assigning back to John the ownership of the house we were living in. But this was not the only stipulation raised in the letter from ABKCO, which read as follows:

It is of course a condition of this arrangement that you withdraw and hand to me for destruction, the statement you have lodged with your solicitor and further that you agree in writing that at no time in the future will you write or give any interviews or do anything of a similar nature relating to your relationship with John.

It seemed to be vitally important that Freddie's lips be kept tightly shut.

The agreement was duly signed and sealed at our solicitor's office in Brighton. We had given strict instructions that our new address was to be kept secret from ABKCO, and as we strolled arm in arm along the seafront, deeply breathing the fresh, salty air, we felt that we had finally cut our links with John.

We now felt ourselves to be reasonably safe from John's wrath, but Freddie had kept a copy of his statement 'just in case'. One could never be too sure of anything where John Lennon was concerned.

It was shortly after we had moved into our seafront flat early in 1971 that Freddie developed an unnaturally ravenous hunger and inexplicable dizzy spells which awoke him at night, leading to a recurrence of the insomnia he had only recently overcome. Later the hospital doctors were to explain these symptoms as the first tell-tale signs of his illness, but we were totally unaware of their significance at the time.

However, there was no doubt in my mind that a worrying change had taken place in the man I loved. His happy-go-lucky outlook and continuous laughing and joking had given way to an out-of-character broodiness, sometimes bordering on depression. Although his ordeal at Ascot still weighed heavily on his mind he scarcely ever spoke of John at this time. In fact it was not until the release of the Imagine album that John's name was mentioned again.

187

In 1971 a new and more outward-looking John Lennon had come into being. With primal therapy well behind him, the introverted self-absorption of the past year had been replaced by a new-found idealism for the brotherhood of man. Having finally shaken off the massive chip upon his shoulder, John now longed to share with the world the peace and understanding which he believed to have found in himself.

Like the rest of John's fans, Freddie was fascinated by the song 'Imagine', which he considered to be a masterpiece – the finest thing that John had ever written. But he was inevitably struck by the apparent hypocrisy of the lyrics. It seemed to him to be almost farcical that John Lennon, 'man of peace', advocate of world unity, was as yet unable to reconcile himself with his father. Yet despite the irony of the situation, this was the only bitter word I heard him utter towards John.

Freddie's rancour was directed almost totally towards Mimi, whom he considered ultimately to blame for the disastrous relationship which now existed between himself and John. Increasingly he came to believe that Mimi had deliberately sought to keep John to herself by contriving to alienate son from father. He held her responsible for thwarting his efforts to reclaim John way back in 1950 by threatening to reveal to John his father's prison record. He also held her responsible for holding back from John vital information which would have given the boy a more positive image of his father. In Freddie's mind it was down to Mimi that John had grown up with the belief that his Dad was a blackguard who cared nothing for his child and had simply deserted him along with his mother. And he believed that John's upbringing had been partly responsible for the psychological turmoil which had led John to Janov therapy and finally to the terrible confrontation with his father.

As far as Freddie was concerned there was no excusing or forgiving Mimi, and he found it impossible to see things from her point of view or to understand the insecurity which motivated her. Of course he was only too well aware that Mimi, at her own admission, had been besotted with John since his birth and had longed to have him as her own child. But what he did not understand was that obsession leads to fear and fear leads to hate. By virtue of his legal right to snatch John from her at any moment, Freddie Lennon had become the secret enemy from whom Mimi felt compelled to defend herself as best she could.

Freddie's recriminations regarding John's mental state were directed not only towards Mimi, however, but towards himself also. John's accusations at Tittenhurst had awakened a sense of personal responsibility for his son's pain. Now for the first time he came to appreciate the implications of his abandonment of John to Mimi: he realized just how deeply John had longed for his father to return, how much he had loved and needed his father, and how he himself had remained tragically unaware of that need. The remorse which now began to engulf Freddie centred not only on the sorrow his absence had caused John during his childhood, but also on the dreadful feeling that he might somehow also be responsible for his son's present 'madness'. It was a heavy burden for any parent to bear.

However, an important means of helping to ease Freddie's anguish was the decision finally to embark on his autobiography, despite John's veto and threats. This was a commitment he had made to himself many years since but which he now felt needed to be put urgently into practice, whatever the consequences.

Given his son's state of mind, Freddie felt it was imperative that John be provided with an accurate account of his father's background, of the events which had unfolded during his childhood, and of the factors which had caused their separation. This, he hoped, would assuage John's hatred and help to calm his tortured recollections of his childhood. For his son's sake and for his own, Freddie believed that it was vitally important that John should now learn the full truth. And it was also essential that our own child should have an accurate account of his father's early life.

Little David had in fact just begun playschool, which gave Freddie a precious three hours every morning at his desk. He found that his powers of recall were remarkably sharp and, with the assistance of a dated record of his career at sea, supplied by the Board of Trade, he constructed a remarkably detailed framework of the main events of his life. The story soon began to take shape in Freddie's dramatic and witty style, and he rediscovered the flair for words previously expressed in flamboyant letters to Julia.

He certainly did seem to have a talent for writing, but, more important still, he thoroughly enjoyed the work. The twelve months or so he spent on his autobiography proved to be excellent therapy. Not only did it help him to take his mind off the morbid happenings of the past year, but it was also a significant way of justifying himself and of relieving his feelings of guilt towards John.

However, finding a suitable agent to handle the sale of the book proved to be much more difficult than either of us had expected, and the verdict of our first approach to the literary world was depressingly unhelpful. 'The problem is that publishers are only interested in John's autobiography,' we were told. 'There just wouldn't be a market for your life story. Perhaps in a few years' time. . . .'

It seemed that the book would just have to wait, and that maybe it would take a little longer than expected before Freddie could finally 'clear his name'.

'But whatever happens, pet,' Freddie insisted, 'you must make sure that John gets to read the book should anything happen to me. Even if the world never gets to know the truth about me, it's vital that John should.'

There and then we made a pact that if the book hadn't been published by the time Freddie died – and in fact we never approached another publisher – then I would ensure without fail that John Lennon received a copy of his father's life story.

Our attention was shortly diverted from the book by a further special blessing from our very own guardian angel. On rereading the lease to our flat, I was staggered to discover our option to purchase the apartment for a figure which was now less than half the market price. This unexpected stroke of good luck supplied us with the deposit for a dear little cottage of our own in a countrified area of Brighton, with a huge, rambling garden for young David to play in.

'You always seem to land on your feet, don't you, pet?' remarked Freddie. 'If you fell down the kazi you'd come up with a rope of pearls around your neck, as my mother Polly used to say.'

Strangely enough, we both felt as if Polly had been helping and guiding us through this difficult period. And the thought began to occur to us that maybe it was indeed Polly who was our guardian angel.

9
LIKE FATHER, LIKE SON

It was while we were living at Blisworth, our idyllic cottage near Brighton, that Freddie began to relax again. Soon the little house was ringing with laughter as he regained his old sense of humour and *joie de vivre*. Like John after him, he had the ability to inspire almost unbearable mirth, and his story-telling had me laughing till my sides ached. But the tales I loved best were those of the old days, tales of Polly and Copperfield Street, which young David, already proud of his heritage, would also avidly absorb.

In October 1973 David was blessed with a little brother, Robin, the child we had been longing for since David's birth in 1969 but which I had experienced difficulty in conceiving. But at last our prayers had been answered, and ironically the baby's 'due date' was quoted as 9 October, promising to coincide with John's birthday. However, for reasons of his own, young Robin was late in arriving and was eventually born on the 22nd. 'It looks as if he's not too keen on sharing a birthday with his elder brother,' commented Freddie drily.

The birth of Robin inevitably resulted in heavier duties for Freddie as house-husband, but these he accepted cheerfully, happy in the knowledge that this time round no one could rebuke him for failing to take his responsibilities as a parent seriously. In fact for the first two years of Robin's life he brought up the little boy virtually single-handed, coping effortlessly with bottle feeding and nappy changing as if born to it.

He became a well-known and popular figure in the

neighbourhood, proudly pushing the baby in his pram, and was accepted with some fascination by the young mothers at the local school where he would call with little Robin to collect David each afternoon.

'Isn't he an absolute corker?' he would gleefully exclaim as passers by stopped to admire the baby, quickly correcting their mistaken assumption that he was referring to his grandson. He may well have been the oldest dad in the district, but he was also most definitely the happiest. And from the number of ice creams young David was able to extract from him he was probably also the most indulgent!

By the autumn of 1975 we were quite simply blissfully happy, leading us to feel that Blisworth had been aptly named for us by the previous owners. We both found it hard to believe that after nearly nine years together such an 'ill-matched' couple as ourselves could still feel so crazy about each other. In fact things were almost dangerously good, and I began to experience ominous premonitions that our happiness simply couldn't continue for long at this level. And sure enough, our peace was shattered by a puzzling message from our solicitor.

'John Lennon has been enquiring about your whereabouts,' he informed us. 'It seems he wishes to contact you urgently – you must decide whether you wish me to divulge your address or not.' This news hit us as something of a bombshell, and for the first time in our new home the name of John Lennon was spoken, reawakening painful memories of our ordeal of five years previously.

As we struggled with the decision as to whether to respond to John's approach, we racked our brains in an effort to assess his motivation. There was always the chance that he might be offering reconciliation, that he wished to stretch out the hand of friendship. But it was equally feasible that he had undergone further therapy and wanted to unleash new-found rage towards his father. I knew that Freddie longed in his heart to be reunited with his first-born, but the risks were so great. It was truly a soul-searching decision.

The year 1975 saw John Lennon as immersed in housewifely duties as his father, although neither was aware of the other's activities. With eighteen months of wild living behind him during his separation from Yoko, John had finally eschewed the vices in order to raise his sperm count and increase Yoko's chances of conceiving a baby. The child they had so long yearned for was finally born on 9 October – presumably happy to share John's birthday, unlike our own son Robin. They named him Sean in the Celtic fashion, reflecting John's preoccupation with his Irish roots, for despite the severing of his links with his family he had enacted during Janov therapy he still felt a fascination with his origins.

This interest in his background was intensified following Sean's birth, giving rise to a need to feel that he 'belonged'. He contacted his two half-sisters, Jackie and Julia, who had been born to his mother and Bobby Dykins and whom he had not seen since 1970 and primal therapy. Becoming a father again seemed to arouse in John the desire for mementoes of his own childhood and his own parents. He spent hours on the transatlantic phone discussing memories of Julia with his two sisters, and constantly pestered them to send him photographs and souvenirs. He also felt the urge to re-establish contact with his father – hence his request to our solicitor for information as to our whereabouts.

John had come a long way since the psychological turmoil of 1970. At last he had kicked the drink and drugs habits to which he had alternately succumbed since long before Beatle days, and just like Freddie, he had been 'on the wagon' since the conception of his new son. Not only was he thinking more clearly than he had for years, but he was also feeling supremely happy and the desire for family unity now transcended his past resentments.

194

Furthermore, his parting from Cynthia and Julian had helped him to realize how easily a man can lose touch with the child of a broken marriage. His tolerance of his own father had taken a giant leap, and the urge to make friends with Freddie was now foremost in his mind.

But despite the uncanny similarity between their life-styles at this time, father and son were totally out of touch with each other. As the two house-husbands immersed themselves in child-rearing and cooking – John baking bread in New York, Freddie changing nappies in Brighton – neither was aware of the other's state of mind. John had no idea at all of the anxiety his request had instilled into his father, or indeed of the pain he had inflicted by his verbal attack five years previously. Freddie for his part had no way of knowing that John's intentions were now friendly and that he meant him no harm. All the worry dating from 1970 was again churned up as we began to fear once more for our own and our children's safety.

'It's no good, darling,' Freddie finally concluded. 'I simply can't take the chance. I just couldn't stand another dose of John's temper. This time I think it really would kill me.'

'Well, in that case we must never see John again,' I agreed and the following day I instructed my solicitor to withhold from John all details of our whereabouts.

It was just three months after John's unexpected approach that Freddie suddenly developed serious problems with his digestion. It all started one Sunday lunchtime when he experienced a cutting pain on swallowing, and within only a couple of weeks he was unable to consume anything at all except liquids. But our greatest cause of alarm was the rapid weight loss which accompanied these symptoms, and which was far in excess of that which would normally result from lack of solid foods.

This sudden turn of events seemed to be almost

unbelievable, particularly since Freddie had hardly had a day sick in his life. By the time we obtained an appointment with a specialist we were both plain scared, and when the doctor gravely announced that urgent hospital tests were necessary, silently we each acknowledged that the good times might be coming to an end.

The prospect of parting seemed terrifying and unbearable. For the last eight years we had lived for each other and the children, never having spent one night apart. As we sat on the bed, reluctantly packing a few items for Freddie's hospital visit, we both broke into sobs and hugged each other in desperation, sensing that our future hung perilously in the balance.

'We're so much a part of each other that I just couldn't cope with losing you now,' whispered Freddie. But somehow he managed to summon up his usual courage and optimism, and valiantly pulling himself together, he urged us to 'stop moping and fight back.'

But despite my efforts to put on a brave face I felt sick and empty inside. It was as if I was living through a nightmare from which I simply couldn't awake. The evening before Freddie was due to go into hospital I was beset by an awful foreboding that this was likely to be our last night together and that Freddie would never come home again.

And although he never expressed his fear that he was suffering from a terminal illness, Freddie himself displayed all the signs of a man who knew the end was near. On that last night he lay awake until the early hours recalling important incidents from the past, discussing and questioning decisions, reliving the major scenarios of his life.

'There's only one thing in my past that I really regret,' he finally admitted as the sun began to rise. It was with some difficulty that he eventually confessed to strong feelings of self-reproach that he had failed to stand up to Mimi and insist on demanding custody of John. He regretted that he had allowed his wounded pride to come between him and his child.

'It was pride which kept me from confronting Julia to demand access to John when she left me for Bobby Dykins. And it was pride which led me to abandon my plan to emigrate with John in case Mimi told him of my prison sentence,' he confided. 'If only I hadn't been so damn big-headed I'd never have let Mimi keep John from me as she did.'

The hopeless conclusions of the hospital tests came as little of a surprise to me. The diagnosis was cancer of the stomach, a grim reflection on Freddie's inability to 'stomach' John's rage which I believe lay at the root of his dis-ease. But although I was prepared for the worst I found it hard to assimilate the doctor's verdict that the condition was undoubtedly terminal.

'We will operate,' he informed me, 'but only in order to alleviate the pain. I'm afraid there's nothing at all we can do to prolong your husband's life.'

I can remember struggling with an overwhelming sense of powerlessness, and desperately resisting acceptance of the unbelievable prognosis. I clung to the hope that a miracle might still be possible and that while Freddie was still alive there was the chance that he might somehow recover. I contacted the Guildford sanctuary of the well-known British spiritual healer Harry Edwards to ask that Freddie's name be added to his absent healing list. They made no promises as to his recovery, but assured me that he would certainly receive help, which eased my mind considerably although I knew the situation to be grave.

It hardly seemed possible that just a few weeks previously Freddie had appeared reasonably fit and healthy, yet when I visited him at the hospital, he already had the look of a man close to death. The flesh had fallen away from him at an alarming speed, leaving him painfully emaciated, and his body had now begun to be racked by sudden excruciating pain.

They were giving him shots of morphine to relieve his distress, but such was the increasing intensity of his pain that he was already dangerously close to the maximum dosage level. As I gazed sadly into his sunken eyes, the pupils contracted under the influence of the narcotics, I was unexpectedly reminded of John and the way he had looked on that terrible day of his thirtieth birthday.

I realized with a jolt that, regardless of my apprehensions of John, I owed it to him to inform him of his father's medical condition, allowing him the opportunity to take whatever action he thought was appropriate before it was finally too late. My phone call to Apple was received by an anxious-sounding and rather curt personal assistant.

'John's been very worried about his father for some time,' she reproached me rather irritably, going on to demand details of Freddie's condition and precise whereabouts. It felt like an interrogation and only added to the stress I was experiencing at the time. But it achieved the desired effect: John made an immediate transatlantic call to his father, which was to lead to their final reconciliation.

At the time of his telephone conversation with his father John was unaware of the terminal nature of his condition. I had merely indicated that Freddie was seriously ill, and it was not until John spoke to the surgeon later that same day that he was to learn that there was no chance of recovery. For this reason there was still hope in his voice as he discussed with his father plans that they would carry out when he was well – plans to see each other again, to talk things out and to forget the past once and for all.

'I read in the papers that you've got the baby you wanted,' said Freddie. 'Guess what – I've got another little lad too, now. He's just two and a half.'

'You cheeky old bastard!' The surprise really registered in John's voice. 'Look, we'll get together just as soon as you're feeling better.' And he dictated his Dakota Mansions phone number to Freddie, urging him to ring him as soon as he was able.

'It'll be great to meet young Sean and to catch up on your music, John – by the way, I loved "Imagine",' was Freddie's delighted response.

The banter, mainly about music, continued along similar lines until John, sensing the tiredness in Freddie's voice, concluded with a cheery 'See you, la,' to which Freddie happily responded, 'See you, la.'

Later that same afternoon the hospital ward was marked by a hushed silence as a huge bouquet arrived by special delivery and was brought in by a somewhat overwhelmed young nurse. 'It's from your son, Mr Lennon,' she gasped as she began to arrange the gloriously coloured sprays on a table at the foot of the bed – the bouquet was too large to fit by the bedside.

It is unlikely that any patient in that hospital had ever received flowers of such quantity or splendour, but for Freddie the most valuable part of the gift was the small card which accompanied it and which bore the words: 'To Dad – Get well soon – With much love from John, Yoko and Sean.' And it was not so much the blooms themselves which caused heads to turn, as the expression of sheer joy on Freddie's face which momentarily helped him to forget the intense pain.

That evening, as I sat on the hospital bed gently holding Freddie's hand, I realized that the bond between us was stronger than ever. It was as though this terrible ordeal had brought us even closer together and our love was somehow reaching a new and higher level. Despite Freddie's haggard appearance his eyes were still beautiful, and their new-found sparkle of excitement made me feel sure that John had at last made his peace.

199

'You'll never guess who phoned me today,' he whispered, with an expression of such relief and happiness that my heart stood still. Despite the sense of numb despair that had been with me ever since Freddie first fell ill, I too almost felt happy as I saw how much the reconciliation meant to him.

Suddenly I realized the depth of his feelings for his son and how much John's anger must have hurt him. Despite our love for each other, and notwithstanding the new family we had raised together, Freddie's anguish over the loss of John, his first-born child, had never left him. And it seemed to me, looking back, that the life force had begun to slip away from him after John's enraged and terrifying outburst towards him.

But although it was now too late for him to recover physically, the light was once again aglow in his eyes and I knew that somehow or other things were OK.

When I next visited Freddie, on what was to prove to be the last evening of his life, he had just come through surgery and was hooked up to various drips and monitors. He had now been transferred from the public ward to an intensive care cubicle. But curiously, despite his pain and discomfort, I felt that his expression was more serene than it had been for many weeks. Able only to murmur one or two breathless words, he turned his eyes to the dazzling floral display which now stood right beside him and then back to me and smiled. This gesture of contentment and the gentle words 'You know I love you', marked Freddie's last moments of consciousness before slipping into a peaceful slumber from which he did not awake.

Before succumbing to the grief which threatened to overwhelm me I was aware that my next task was to ensure that John received his father's autobiography, written back in 1971 to refute the ill-founded stories about Freddie which had appeared in the media since John's rise to fame.

'Promise me one thing, pet,' Freddie had asked of me at that time. 'When I'm gone, make sure that John gets to read

200

the book. Make sure he finally gets to know the truth about his dad.'

There were also other factors to take into account. Our own two sons would undoubtedly be anxious to learn about the true identity of their father when he was dead – and sadly the odds had always dictated that by virtue of Freddie's age he wouldn't be around when they were grown-up. So for their sake also, we had felt that an accurate account of the truth was needed.

'It's up to you now, darling,' Freddie had announced on completing the manuscript. 'It'll be your task to clear my name – the book will prove everything.' I knew in my bones that one day it would indeed fall upon me to put things straight. Now that time had arrived.

Putting the final touches to Freddie's manuscript, having it photocopied and packing it for despatch to New York used up all of the little energy I had left after Freddie's death. But within a week it was on its way to John, together with the following letter, written in 1971, in which Freddie spoke heart-to-heart to his son in a way he had never been able to during his lifetime:

Dear John,

By the time you read this letter I will already be dead, but I hope it will not be too late to fill the gaps in your knowledge of your old man which have caused you distress throughout your life.

Despite your undoubted talents, your memories of your childhood appear to be non-existent, and so I hope the reading of my story will help you to establish what really happened in those early years. Of course, your only source of information has been your Aunt Mimi who for reasons best known to herself refrained from telling you anything about me. Consequently, as in Hunter Davies's biography of the Beatles, it wasn't so much what was said about me but rather what was left unsaid that caused you so much embarrassment and pain.

Since last we met on the occasion of your thirtieth birthday I have been haunted by the image of you screaming for your Daddy and it is my sincere hope that when you have read this book you will no longer bear me any malice. Perhaps the revelations in my life story may bring you a clearer picture of how fate and circumstance control so much of our lives and therefore must be considered in our judgement of one another.

Until we meet again, some time, some place,

Your Father,
Freddie Lennon

I was hopeful that Freddie's wish would be fulfilled and that, having read the book, John would have a better understanding of his father, even if it were too late for them to enjoy the fruits of that understanding. But on the exit of one Lennon, another had entered the world, and with the birth of his son Sean six months previously John was able to lavish on the child all the love which had never been allowed to express itself for his father. It seemed to be a question of a life for a life, and interestingly it was not long before Sean Lennon began to manifest much of the high spirits and sense of humour of his Irish forebears, and in particular his grandfather Freddie.

When Freddie's old pal Tony Cartwright arrived to escort me to the funeral, his comment on the offer I had received from John to pay his father's cremation costs was scathing and to the point.

'I'd have told the bastard what he could do with his bloody money,' he said.

Tony had made a name for himself in showbiz and was managing several successful acts, but he had not forgotten his first prodigy. Fellow Scousers, Tony and Freddie had felt a deep and lasting affection for each other which had led them to keep in touch since 1966 after Freddie had quit the pop world. As Tony saw things, Freddie had received a raw deal at the hands both of John and the press, who had mercilessly dragged his name through the mud.

'It's a bloody shame,' he repeated over and over again as we drove to the crematorium in the hired limousine, commiserating over our dear friend's extraordinarily fated life which had so abruptly come to an end.

Tony was possibly the only person apart from me with whom Freddie had felt able to be 'himself' in recent years, and we both loved him dearly. We contemplated with mixed feelings the elaborate and expensive wreath which had been delivered on behalf of John, Yoko and Sean, who could not have attended the funeral even if they had wished to since John was still confined to the USA awaiting the issue of his residence permit, known as a Green Card. We spent the remainder of the afternoon reminiscing over the good times we had both enjoyed with Freddie.

'He was just such good fun to be with,' commented Tony. 'I used to call him the oldest teenager in the world'. It seemed strangely appropriate that he had died on 1 April – April Fools' Day. Throughout his life he had clowned and joked and generally acted the fool. And it seemed to me that at times life had done a pretty good job of making a perfect fool of him.

As I sat weeping over his memory, Tony reminded me that Freddie would not have wished to see me this way, and I felt as if I could hear his voice urging me to be brave and hold back the tears. I remembered the words of the song 'Smile Though Your Heart Is Aching', an old favourite of Freddie's which had seen him through the many traumas in his own life. As Tony assured me that it would be possible for me to begin my life anew, I felt certain that if I 'smiled through the tears and sorrow' then one day soon I would 'see the sun come shining through'.

The day on which John Lennon received the bulky brown package which contained his father's manuscript was of great importance in his life. As he thumbed slowly through the pages of the one hundred and fifty thousand word text, with little else to occupy him at the Dakota at that time, he was able to spend long hours poring over the story of his early childhood, filling in the gaps in Mimi's carefully vetted account.

Now at last he came to realize just how much Freddie had loved Julia and how hard he had tried to save his marriage despite her adultery. Most importantly he came to understand that his father had cared deeply for him and had made great efforts to obtain custody of his son – until he was defeated by Mimi.

Now too the enigmatic personality of the wayward Freddie came vividly to life for him for the very first time. His previous image of his father as the ne'er-do-well his aunt had described or the footloose and fancy-free sailor of his childhood fantasies now became slowly replaced by a four-square picture of a man with a hatred of convention and establishment values just like himself, with strong ideals and principles just like himself, and with a deep sensitivity which he attempted to conceal, as John did, behind a sharp tongue and a sharp wit.

It was not only the similarity between their respective personalities which made such a deep impression on John. The further he read, progressing from one fateful episode to the next, the more he became aware of the uncanny parallels between the two men's life patterns – of their tendency to react to blows or disappointments by lashing out violently without regard for the consequences to others or themselves, and then retreat; and of their tendency to blot out their emotional pain through alcohol or drugs.

Each exhibited a frightening ability to cut himself off ruthlessly, as a consequence of his anger, from people with whom they had been long involved. It was this tendency that caused Freddie to sever his links with Julia and John, and later with his brother Sydney. It was the same tendency which led John to end virtually all contact with Cynthia and Julian after his divorce, and later to break so bitterly from Paul McCartney and many other close associates.

There was little doubt in John's mind that he had inherited his wandering spirit from his father – his inability to accept the status quo or lead a mundane existence. He was fascinated to discover the two shared passions – the sea and the stage – which had dominated each of their lives. Freddie had been frustrated in his attempts at a stage career and subsequently turned to his second love, ships. And before he dedicated himself to rock and roll, John had been mesmerized by the sea: together with Pete Shotton he had attempted to enlist at the Merchant Navy school in Liverpool – until he was stopped by Mimi.

But more than anything else, it was the common ambivalence towards fatherhood which struck a deep chord within John. For despite his criticism of Freddie for his neglect of him as a youngster, it slowly dawned upon John that he had found it just as difficult to carry out his own fatherly duties towards Julian, a child towards whom he felt no paternal instincts whatsoever. Indeed it now seemed to him that he himself had in effect abandoned Julian when he divorced Cynthia for Yoko, virtually severing all contact with the lad until urged by his lover, May Pang, to invite Julian to the States for a mutually embarrassing and stressful visit.

Certainly, both Freddie and John had been denied a father role-model, each having lost his father, the one by death and the other by separation, at approximately the same age. And perhaps it was for this reason – coupled with a strong need for independence and an aversion to domesticity – that they had both found it so difficult to assume the father role themselves.

But whatever their psychological motives, the similarity

between the two men's approach towards their first sons was striking. And despite John Lennon's lifelong criticism of his father, he now came to see that his own behaviour towards Julian was the very thing he had condemned in Freddie. Anxious to atone for his cruel treatment of Julian, John hit upon two plans of action to make amends – and here, once again, he followed in his father's footsteps.

In reading Freddie's account of his later years, John had been impressed by his father's dedication to the rearing of his young sons, David and Robin, as a means of compensating for his failure with John. True, even before he learned of Freddie's transformation to domesticity, John had already decided to spend as much time as possible with little Sean. But now, as he came to understand the tremendous sense of expiation which Freddie had experienced by his devotion to his children, *total* commitment to Sean became essential in John's eyes. This would be a means whereby he too could relieve his guilty conscience. It would also be a means of redeeming the karma which he believed lay behind his own painful childhood. So it was that, like Freddie before him, John was to assume the role of house-husband, although perhaps with a little more paid help than his father had enjoyed.

It was also of vital importance to John that Julian should somehow be provided with a better image of him as a father than the image he himself had carried of Freddie for most of his life. John was especially afraid that after his death – and he lived his last years in constant anticipation of an early death – Julian would have no memory of his father other than painful recollections of his neglect and harsh treatment. This was of particular concern to John in view of the pain he had suffered through his feelings about Freddie.

However, by reading Freddie's life story his outlook on his father had been totally turned around, and he had come to understand Freddie in a way which otherwise would have been impossible. And as he gained insight into the complexities of his father's character and the fateful circumstances which had overshadowed their relationship, his understanding blossomed into compassion and he felt true forgiveness. Ironically, the same book which six years ago he had forbidden his father to write on pain of death now brought him new peace of mind.

It struck John that if he in turn could provide Julian with a similar chronicle, to be passed to him on his own death, Julian might come to experience similar understanding and forgiveness of the way John had treated him as a child. He was struck also by the opportunity that such a chronicle would provide for him to discharge his deepest feelings and beliefs to his son – just as Freddie had done in his autobiography – unhampered by the self-consciousness that person-to-person contact might produce.

In 1975 John had begun to keep a personal journal. Now, after reading Freddie's life story, he resolved to dedicate this journal to Julian and to offer it to him on his own death. As a record of his day-to-day existence, it would, he hoped, have the same effect on Julian as Freddie's book had had on him.

The personal assistant and companion with whom John had discussed his impressions of his seafaring father Freddie was the uncannily aptly named Fred Seaman. This sensitive young man was John's only close friend towards the end of his life and thus it was natural that he should talk at length with Seaman about his reaction to his father's life story and his anxieties regarding Julian. It was to Seaman that John entrusted the vital task of ensuring that in the event of his death his personal journal should safely reach Julian's hands.

And it was with the help of Fred Seaman – again perfectly befitting his name – that John finally confronted his love/hate relationship with the sea. Since early childhood the ocean had held a romantic fascination for John as the means whereby Freddie had escaped from Liverpool to live a life of freedom and adventure and John in turn had

207

yearned to follow his father's example and himself run away to sea.

But at the same time John had long harboured feelings of fear and resentment towards the sea for having stolen his father from him – feelings which he now overcame with Fred Seaman's encouragement. At Seaman's suggestion he set sail for the first time, initially in a small boat off Long Island and later, in June 1980, he joined the crew of a schooner bound for Bermuda.

During a violent storm, as one member of the crew after another fell victim to sea sickness, John was summoned from the galley to take the helm, and for a couple of hours he found himself master of the ship. As the huge menacing waves crashed towards him, all his old feelings of excitement and fear came surging up inside him. But this time he was completely in control, and gradually he came to feel strangely confident and secure. Finally, as the realization hit him that the sea was no longer his enemy, John experienced a sense of profound inner calm.

In making his peace with the sea, he had taken the final step in freeing himself of the pain associated with his boyhood parting from Freddie. By the time of his murder in December 1980 perhaps John Lennon had at last come to terms with the father whom he had loved and lost, whom he had idolized and despised, and whose life pattern he had eventually come to recognize as a mirror image of his own.

SELECT BIBLIOGRAPHY

Jann Wenner – Lennon Remembers: The Rolling Stone Interviews with John Lennon and Yoko Ono (Penguin 1973);

Albert Goldman – The Lives of John Lennon (Bantam Press 1988);

Ray Connolly – John Lennon 1940–1980, A Biography (Fontana 1981);

Pete Shotton and Nicholas Schaffner – John Lennon In My Life (Coronet 1984).